Alphabet Stitchery
by Hand
and Machine

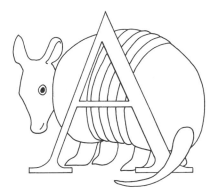

OTHER BOOKS AVAILABLE FROM CHILTON
Robbie Fanning, Series Editor

CONTEMPORARY QUILTING

Barbara Johannah's Crystal Piecing
The Complete Book of Machine Quilting, Second Edition, by Robbie and Tony Fanning
Contemporary Quilting Techniques, by Pat Cairns
Creative Triangles for Quilters, by Janet B. Elwin
Fast Patch, by Anita Hallock
Fourteen Easy Baby Quilts, by Margaret Dittman
Machine-Quilted Jackets, Vests, and Coats, by Nancy Moore
Pictorial Quilts, by Carolyn Vosburg Hall
Precision Pieced Quilts Using the Foundation Method, by Jane Hall and Dixie Haywood
Quick-Quilted Home Decor with Your Bernina, by Jackie Dodson
Quick-Quilted Home Decor with Your Sewing Machine, by Jackie Dodson
The Quilter's Guide to Rotary Cutting, by Donna Poster
Scrap Quilts Using Fast Patch, by Anita Hallock
Shirley Botsford's Daddy's Ties
Speed-Cut Quilts, by Donna Poster
Stitch 'n' Quilt, by Kathleen Eaton
Super Simple Quilts, by Kathleen Eaton
Teach Yourself Machine Piecing and Quilting, by Debra Wagner
Three-Dimensional Appliqué, by Jodie Davis
Three-Dimensional Pieced Quilts, by Jodie Davis

CRAFT KALEIDOSCOPE

Creating and Crafting Dolls, by Eloise Piper and Mary Dilligan
Fabric Crafts and Other Fun with Kids, by Susan Parker Beck and Charlou Lunsford
Fabric Painting Made Easy, by Nancy Ward
Jane Asher's Costume Book
Quick and Easy Ways with Ribbon, by Ceci Johnson
Learn Bearmaking, by Judi Maddigan
Soft Toys for Babies, by Judi Maddigan
Stamping Made Easy, by Nancy Ward
Too Hot To Handle? Potholders and How to Make Them, by Doris L. Hoover

CREATIVE MACHINE ARTS

ABCs of Serging, by Tammy Young and Lori Bottom
The Button Lover's Book, by Marilyn Green
Claire Shaeffer's Fabric Sewing Guide
The Complete Book of Machine Embroidery, by Robbie and Tony Fanning
Creative Nurseries Illustrated, by Debra Terry and Juli Plooster
Distinctive Serger Gifts and Crafts, by Naomi Baker and Tammy Young
Friendship Quilts by Hand and Machine, by Carolyn Vosburg Hall
Gail Brown's All-New Instant Interiors
Hold It! How to Sew Bags, Totes, Duffels, Pouches, and More, by Nancy Restuccia

How to Make Soft Jewelry, by Jackie Dodson
Innovative Serging, by Gail Brown and Tammy Young
Innovative Sewing, by Gail Brown and Tammy Young
Jan Saunders' Wardrobe Quick-Fixes
The New Creative Serging Illustrated, by Pati Palmer, Gail Brown, and Sue Green
Petite Pizzazz, by Barb Griffin
Putting on the Glitz, by Sandra L. Hatch and Ann Boyce
Quick Napkin Creations, by Gail Brown
Second Stitches: Recycle as You Sew, by Susan Parker
Serge a Simple Project, by Tammy Young and Naomi Baker
Serge Something Super for Your Kids, by Cindy Cummins
Sew Any Patch Pocket, by Claire Shaeffer
Sew Any Set-In Pocket, by Claire Shaeffer
Sew Sensational Gifts, by Naomi Baker and Tammy Young
Sewing and Collecting Vintage Fashions, by Eileen MacIntosh
Simply Serge Any Fabric, by Naomi Baker and Tammy Young
Soft Gardens: Make Flowers with Your Sewing Machine, by Yvonne Perez-Collins
The Stretch & Sew Guide to Sewing Knits, by Ann Person
Twenty Easy Machine-Made Rugs, by Jackie Dodson

KNOW YOUR SEWING MACHINE SERIES,
by Jackie Dodson

Know Your Bernina, second edition
Know Your Brother, with Jane Warnick
Know Your New Home, with Judi Cull and Vicki Lyn Hastings
Know Your Pfaff, with Audrey Griese
Know Your Sewing Machine
Know Your Singer
Know Your Viking, with Jan Saunders
Know Your White, with Jan Saunders

KNOW YOUR SERGER SERIES,
by Tammy Young and Naomi Baker

Know Your baby lock
Know Your Serger
Know Your White Superlock

STARWEAR

Embellishments, by Linda Fry Kenzle
Make It Your Own, by Lori Bottom and Ronda Chaney
Mary Mulari's Garments with Style
Pattern-Free Fashions, by Mary Lee Trees Cole
Shirley Adams' Belt Bazaar
Sweatshirts with Style, by Mary Mulari

TEACH YOURSELF TO SEW BETTER,
by Jan Saunders

A Step-by-Step Guide to Your Bernina
A Step-by-Step Guide to Your New Home
A Step-by-Step Guide to Your Sewing Machine
A Step-by-Step Guide to Your Viking

Alphabet Stitchery by Hand and Machine

CAROLYN VOSBURG HALL

CHILTON BOOK COMPANY
Radnor, Pennsylvania

Published in Radnor, Pennsylvania 19089,
by Chilton Book Company

Cover Design by Anthony Jacobson

Interior Design by Stan Green/Green Graphics

Photographs by Carolyn Vosburg Hall,
unless otherwise noted

Color photographs by Donna H. Chiarelli

Line drawings by Carolyn Vosburg Hall

Manufactured in the United States of America

Library of Congress Cataloging in Publication Data
Hall, Carolyn Vosburg
    Alphabet stitchery by hand and machine / Carolyn Vosburg Hall.
      p. cm. — (Creative machine arts)
    Includes bibliographical references and index.
    ISBN 0-8019-8527-7 (pb)
    1. Needlework—Patterns. 2. Alphabets in art. 3. Embroidery,
Machine. 4. Lettering. I. Title. II. Series: Creative machine
arts series.
TT753.H35 1995   95-32736
746.4—dc20   CIP

1 2 3 4 5 6 7 8 9 0   4 3 2 1 9 8 7 6 5

Contents

Cackle, Cackle, Mother Goose, Have you any feathers loose? Truly have I, Pretty Fellow. Half enough to fill a pillow. Here is down, Collect some, do. It can make a quilt for you.

Carolyn Hall 1984

Acknowledgments

Thanks first to Robbie Fanning, series editor, who is always a source of new ideas, bubbly encouragement, country-wide sewing contacts, and general assistance to me—and so many others. Robbie prompted a bonanza for me to test top-of-the-line computer sewing machines—miraculous devices that can embroider professional-quality lettering. Thanks to Brother, Bernina, Elna, New Home, Pfaff, and Viking sewing machine companies for creating these machines and allowing me to try them and produce several projects for this book. Thanks to Sulky for all the wonderful colors of thread to experiment with—I feel rich! I can't miss thanking the many people at Chilton, such as editor Kathy Conover, who helped make this book a reality. And thanks to Barbara Ellis for careful and inspired editing to polish the result.

—Carolyn Vosburg Hall

I-1. Novelty Alphabet. The twenty-six letters of our alphabet can appear in a bewildering variety of shapes, forms, and sizes, from straightforward and utilitarian to simply fanciful. Which style of lettering will suit your stitchery idea?

Introduction

Have you noticed that the quilts, stitchery projects, and clothing we make and buy are often embellished with symbols or letters? Symbols are everywhere carrying their messages. Look around, and you're sure to spot an embroidered lazy daisy, the abstract Flying Geese quilt pattern, or some combination of our twenty-six letter alphabet. All communicate a message—either with words, symbols, or a combination of the two—and we can read them all. My children learned to read in the supermarket by looking at pictures of food accompanied by familiar brand logos and actual words on cereal boxes.

This book presents ways to stitch letters, words, monograms, and sayings—often combined with pictures—using a variety of materials and techniques. You'll find ideas and information on everything from using cut-out cloth letters to the cutting-edge computerized sewing machines, which will sew letters and images for you. I have included projects that range from decorating existing objects in a few minutes to sewing time-consuming patchwork quilts—you will find a whole host of easier and quicker projects in between. You can follow the step-by-step directions and illustrations to make any of the more than twenty projects shown. You will also find loads of suggestions for adapting the projects to suit your taste.

Letters in stitchery not only send messages, they are design objects in and of themselves. Throughout the book, you will find tips and techniques for making attractive lettering and using it effectively. Every chapter has at least one featured Alphabet Page you can adapt and use for your own projects. Some of the featured typefaces are centuries old; others are brand-new and were created specifically for this book. You will also learn how to create your own type styles. One trip to the public library will provide you with literally hundreds more to use. There, you will find calligraphy and typography books with many letter style examples to borrow. (The best tool for "harvesting" lettering is the photocopy machine.) You will also find letters to use in art and craft stores, which carry instant lettering in a variety of typefaces to press on paper or iron on fabric. These stores will also have stencils to trace, stipple, or spray paint letters.

Throughout the book I also have included suggestions and ideas for creating effective designs. The more attention you give to design—the choice of colors in thread and fabric, and the innovative use of lettering—the better your project will turn out. I hope this information will help you learn to trust your own intuition on what style of lettering best expresses your idea, or what striking contrast you might employ.

You will find a summary of topics, along with a list of projects and featured alphabets, on the Contents page. For some instant inspiration, turn to the Color Section of the book to see many of the projects in full color. You will also find photographs of several "Guest Artist" pieces that illustrate some of the many directions alphabet stitchery can take. Or simply page through the book looking for ideas you would like to try.

I hope the projects, patterns, lettering styles, tips, and techniques in this book will be a jumping off point for you. All of the information is designed to help you find new and exciting ways to communicate your own messages. I hope it serves as a treasure-trove of ideas for years to come, and sends you searching for new ways to incorporate words and letters in your stitchery. So turn the page, and let's have some fun with alphabet stitchery!

1-1. This verbal/visual self portrait, titled I Am What I Think, *features machine-programmed letters sewn in a variety of colors on a variety of fabrics.*

CHAPTER ONE

About Lettering

Letters of the alphabet are the most common design symbols we see everyday—on cereal boxes, street signs, television, as well as in books and magazines. All letters have character, no matter what the shape and size. Ones with wide strokes are like hefty football players; slender letters resemble fashion models. Medium-thick letters are sturdy and solid, like workhorses. This chapter is an introduction to letters, because knowing a bit about them will help you use them effectively to express yourself in stitchery. There are literally hundreds of types and styles of letters you can use in stitchery. You will find many examples of different types of letters, along with different ways to use them in projects, throughout this book.

Lettering Basics

Whether you are decorating kid's clothes with letters or using words to make an art quilt, creating attractive and effective lettering is important. Plan to give your lettering personality. Your handwriting has it, and your printing will, too.

Letters are made of strokes. Grab a marker and print "**HELP!**" and you use strong strokes to form the letters. Print "𝔚𝔈𝔏𝔠𝔬𝔪𝔈" and you add finishing lines to the strokes called serifs. Make a sign saying "**GARAGE SALE**" and you will use bold letters for visibility. Invitation lettering can be delicate and rhythmic—"*PLEASE COME*," for example.

When you plan a project, decide what effect you want your stitchery to have—casual or formal, precise or cluttered, playful or serious, simple or elegant—and choose a lettering style that fits. Keep in mind that details matter. Make sure words are spelled right and grammar is correct. Form the letters correctly—no backward "N"s or "S"s. Aim to arrange the lettering and related artwork into a pleasing design and make sure the lettering reads well.

Professional graphic designers can make up spellings, fool with letter shapes, and make reading the words a puzzle, but they have lots of experience and, undoubtedly, a further goal in mind for doing this—to appear childlike, exaggerate shapes, or engage your attention. It's best to keep your designs simple and straightforward before you begin experimenting.

Types of Letters

Our Arabic alphabet has evolved over the years from pictographs, to symbols, to letter characters. Each was refined in relation to the tools used to form them. Japanese and Chinese characters show their origin in brush marks. Roman, the most commonly used typeface for books and newspapers, was originally carved in stone (see Fig. 1-2). Now hundreds of variations are available for us to use.

Five basic categories of lettering have evolved. Each has a name, but as with quilt patterns, this sometimes varies with circumstances. In printing they are

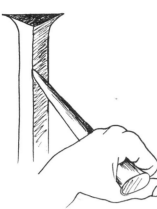

1-2. Roman type was originally chiseled in stone. Serifs, the horizontal strokes at the ends of the letters, originated when carvers chiseled finishing details on letters.

Roman
Gothic
Old English
Italic
Script

Roman
Block
Gothic
Italic
Script

1-3. Five basic type styles, called typefaces in printing (above left) and styles in hand lettering (above right), have evolved. They have different names based on how the letters were originally formed.

called typefaces and have one set of names; when hand lettered by a calligrapher, they are called styles and have a different set of names (see Fig. 1-3).

Roman. Roman is the most common type style used today. Its thick and thin strokes were originally carved in stone (See Fig. 1-2) and finished with serifs—a chiseled cross stroke to refine the stroke ends.

Block or Gothic. Letters with strokes all the same width evolved from the lettering Goths, a Germanic people, made when marking with a stick in clay. This style is called Gothic in printed type, and Block in hand lettering. Hand embroidery or patchwork letters are often done with block letters.

Old English or Gothic. Before printed text and cursive writing, this lettering was done by monks with wide-stroke quill pens on parchment manuscripts. In the late 1400s Gutenberg invented the first movable printing-press type based on this style. This style is called Old English in printed type, and Gothic when hand lettered.

Italic. This style was developed in the 16th century to write more quickly. Italic letters have slanted, softer lines derived from the righthand slant of the hand-written strokes in clay tablets.

Script. Script letters are connected and may be straight or slanted, delicate or bold. Italics joined together formed script, our contemporary handwriting. This style can be simple or wonderfully elaborate.

Letter Style Variations

The basic shapes of letters, including their form, size, and visual weight, can be changed to create different effects. The manner in which each letter is created, or executed, is also important. Spacing and layout also are important ways to create effects.

Form. There are endless variations for each typeface or style—wider strokes, added swashes, rounder corners, altered shape. For example, Fig. 1-4 shows just some of the variations of a block typeface called Helvetica. All type styles have names, including those used in the projects in this book. You'll find a variety of them on

the Alphabet Pages in each chapter of this book. Some are existing styles; others were developed for this book. You can use existing

Helvetica Thin
Helvetica Light
Helvetica
Helvetica Medium
Helvetica Medium
Helvetica Bold
Helvetica Bold Out.
Helvetica Ultra Black
Helvetica Light Italic
Helvetica Italic
Helvetica Italic Out.
Helvetica Medium Italic
Helvetica Medium Flair
Helvetica Bold Italic
Helvetica Reg.

1-4. Each typeface can have many variations. This example shows the variations of the typeface called Helvetica. Notice how the width, size, and thickness of the lines vary. There are also versions with italic and decorative letters.

1-5. Most type styles have capital and small letters that align horizontally on guide lines. Ascenders extend above the main guide line; descenders extend below the base line.

type styles or design your own lettering following basic elements.

Size. Most type styles have larger capital, or uppercase, letters and smaller lowercase letters. Lowercase letters are usually ⅔ the height of the capital letters, but even this can vary with some typefaces. Fig. 1-5 shows the relationship of letter sizes in a classic roman typeface. Type set in all capital letters is generally harder to read than type set with capital and lowercase letters.

Type comes in various sizes, too, from tiny telephone book print to supermarket banners. In printed typefaces the size of the letters is designated by points. For example, the words you are reading in this book are set in 11 point type The chapter titles are set in 68 point type, and the head at the beginning of the chapter

1-6. This cross-stitch letter, designed by Mary Zee, uses thick and thin strokes to create the letter, which is also embellished with a flower motif.

"Lettering Basics" is set in 18 point type.

Weight. Letters made with wide strokes look heavier than ones made with thin ones. Block letters, which are made with strokes of all the same thickness, can look light or heavy, depending on the width of the stroke. Stroke width can vary from thin to thick within each letter in other type styles (see Fig. 1-6). In addition, the proportion of each letter can be varied to better fit spaces—the shape of an "O" can be enlarged into a broad, fat shape or reduced to a narrow oval, for example. You will find examples of how designers have used various types to fit various spaces in nearly any magazine.

Execution. This refers to how the letters are formed and how they relate to one another. To evaluate the execution of the letters in a project, ask yourself if all the letters are beautifully formed and ideally related to one another and the design. Attention to details makes a difference. Are they all formed correctly, with no backward letters, misspelled words, and no mix of upper-and lowercase letters unless intended? If the letters aren't exquisite are they consistent? Making letters is a demanding business. We see so much effective lettering in magazines, posters, books and on television that our eyes demand it even on quilts and T-shirts. If your hand lettering doesn't make the

grade borrow some, by tracing and enlarging one of the alphabets in this book.

Spacing. The spacing between letters and lines of words is just as important as the formation of letters themselves. Words with close intervals between letters and wider spaces between words are easiest to read. (In the text you are reading, the letter "i" is given less space than "m" to make it easier to read, for example.) On older typewriters all letters were spaced the same distance apart, resulting in a slightly clumsy look.

Vertical spacing between lines of lettering affects readability, too. Usually, lines of type are spaced closer together than the height of the letters, because that makes them easier to read and take in the message. In justified text, letters line up to the edge on both right and left margins. This can result in hyphenated words and unequal spacing between words. (Many newspapers are set using this style.) Avoid hyphens to make your messages easier to read. When you design, experiment with arranging and shifting letters and words to get the best effects.

Layout. Type is easiest to read when it is arranged in straight lines, and people expect to find it so. Lettering in English and European language usually reads from left to right, and words or letters are more difficult to decipher if they are arranged vertically or are or stair-stepped.

The way letters, words, and phrases are arranged on the background creates different effects. For an informal or casual quality, use your own handwriting or lettering, and let it ramble along as it goes. Formal calligraphy requires more precision. To evaluate your layout, squint your eyes to see if the overall design is effective for your purposes. To judge the

1-7. When drawing guide lines or straight lines for letters, use a drawing board equipped with a movable straight-edge or T-square. For curves, use a compass, a circle guide, a French curve, or a flexible guide. Use a protractor for drawing script or italic angles.

words, imagine singing the layout. Is it cohesive, sensible, rhythmic with accents and lulls?

Making and Using Letters

This book explains how to design some of the types used in projects so you can create your own type styles, but it is far easier to copy the type styles provided. You can use the type style given for a particular project for many different purposes: embroider the cut-out letter shapes, paint the appliquéd ones, or monogram with whatev-

er type style you wish.

Ready-made letters are another good source of letters to use for projects. Art or craft stores carry instant lettering in a variety of typefaces to press on paper or iron on fabric. (Press-type, Letra-set, and Chartpak are three types.) These stores will also have lettering stencils to trace or paint through, stamps to print, and screen printing supplies. Or you can free-hand squeeze paint on fabric, a quick but messy technique. Squeeze paint is especially fun to use on T-shirts.

The amazing computer-programmed sewing machines allow

you to embroider in a variety of type styles and sizes as well. (Mine has about 6 fonts or kinds of type.) They are expensive and a bit fussy, but the results are remarkable. Chapter 5 showcases several of these marvelous machines loaned to me by generous sewing machine companies. Use these when possible as a basis for your lettering.

If you plan to use lettering from other sources, a photocopy machine is your best tool for harvesting the different type styles that appeal to you from various sources. It's relatively easy to find copiers that enlarge, reduce, or

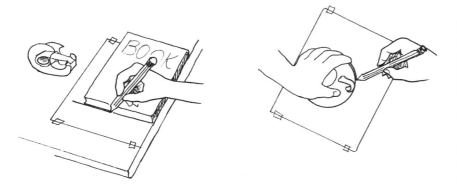

1-8. If you don't have drafting tools, you can draw straight guide lines with a book or magazine squared up with a table edge to simulate a T-square. Use a roll of tape, a cup, or a plate to trace even circles and curves.

print in color, putting lettering designed over the ages at your disposal. To find different styles to use, look at lettering and typography books at your public library or art and office supply stores. In addition, you will find interesting type in books and magazines of all kinds.

Tools and Supplies for Making Letters

You need drafting tools and supplies to help make neat lettering (see Fig. 1-7). The list below gives you the basic supplies to keep on hand.

Paper. To try out ideas and trace letters, sketch or tracing paper is ideal. Use inexpensive photocopy paper or plain newsprint (it comes in pads) to make patterns and stabilize fabrics. Heavier paper or stiff plastic is suitable for making templates. Graph paper is useful for measuring and devising lettering.

Markers. Use a sharp No. 2 pencil to draw lightly on the back of fabric, and a gum eraser, even on fabrics. Mark seam lines on the back of the fabric with pencil, colored pencil, or tailor's chalk. Few markers are really permanent for lettering on fabric except a few

indelible markers or the new fabric-paint markers. Water-based marker ink will bleed, so don't use it for seam lines or pattern outlines. Some marker inks are designed to disappear in time or with washing.

Tapes. Masking tape is useful for holding paper steady. Use clear tape to hold fabrics in appliqué and duct tape to square up a quilt face.

Tools. To make horizontal and vertical lines accurately, a T-square is useful. Use a triangle to establish straight, evenly spaced lines; even better, use a drawing board with a movable straight edge. Use a scale ruler or tape for measuring. Draw curved letters with a compass, plastic circle guides, a French curve, or flexible curve guide. Use a light box (or window and daylight) for tracing and a photocopier for borrowing type.

If you don't want to invest in drafting tools, you can draw horizontal guide lines using a book or magazine squared up with the straight edge of a table. Tape paper to the table lined up with the right edge and mark where you want guide lines. Slide the book or magazine along the paper, keeping it square with the table edge, and draw lines along the top edge across the paper at your marks (see Fig. 1-8).

Drawing Letters

To draw a set of letters on paper, establish a top, bottom, and center guide line for height just like those green-lined practice sheets you toiled over in the grade school (see Fig. 1-9). Slide the right-angle triangle along the base line to make letters straight up and down. Italic letters all slant to the same degree, so to draw italic letters, draw angled guide lines all

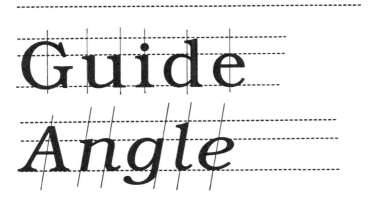

1-9. Guide lines will help you draw accurate, consistent letters. The center guide line is usually two-thirds up from the bottom line (top). Vertical strokes along the line will help you draw letters that are straight up and down (center). For italic lettering, draw angled strokes to keeps the same consistent slant (bottom).

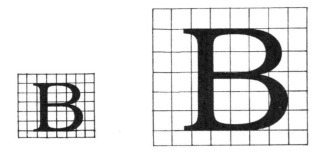

1-10. One way to scale up letters and other images to size is by using the traditional grid method. Just copy the lines in each square of a smaller grid onto the equivalent squares of a larger grid. Enlarging on a photocopier is more accurate and much less work.

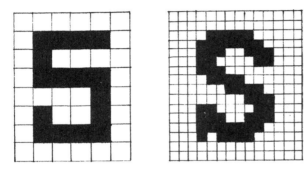

1-11. When graphing letters, the smaller the grid, the closer you can get to smooth curves. The "S" on the large grid (left) has minimal detail, but on a smaller grid (right) it is possible to achieve more shape.

1-12. Every Silver Lining Has A Cloud *is a cross-stitch project you can make using the chart provided in this chapter.*

CLOUD CROSS-STITCH

Overview. Cross-stitch can be used as a way of graphing lettering and artwork, as well as to reproduce it in sewing. This is one of the most portable of crafts. Store the project in a plastic zip bag and take it everywhere. Mine went on a cruise.

Technique. Cross-stitch by hand.

Type style. Block letters are perfect for graphed projects like cross-stitch or needlepoint. See Fig. 1-13 for the entire alphabet.

Size. Design area 6½" X 9" (16.5cm X 23cm), 2 strands of floss on 14-count fabric.

Color concept. Letters are dark on a light background and change to silver letters on a dark background.

the same angle. Even if you are working with ready-made letters you will probably need a base guide line.

It helps to trace a set of letters to become familiar with their shapes. Some capital letters will exceed the top line and go below the bottom line, since round letters need to be slightly taller to appear the same size. Several lowercase letters descend below the line and ascend above the center line. You will find information on special characteristics of featured type styles throughout this book.

Scaling and Transferring

How can any artist exist without the use of a photocopy machine these days? We indulged ourselves with one when my husband

retired, and find we use it almost daily for one thing or another. I wish we had gotten one that scaled things up and down in size. A photocopy machine is a very easy way to enlarge or reduce letters and is more accurate than scaling up by graphing. You can also make accurate lettering of various sizes by computer. Lacking either wonder toy, you can project the lettering by slide projector or magic lantern (overhead projector or children's toy projector) onto guide lines drawn on paper. Trace the projected image and use drafting tools to make the letter shapes true.

Tracing or drawing letters directly on graph paper with its measured lines is a simple and straightforward way to create neat even lettering. You can measure

ABCDEFG HIJKLMN OPQRSTU VWXYZ & abcdefghi jklmnopqr stuvwxyz

1-13. Helvetica Bold Alphabet. Use these bold-style letters for tracing, enlarging, or as a guide to make your own letters. Notice that strokes on the capital letters are all the same thickness. Strokes on lowercase letters are all the same thickness except where a loop joins an upright ("b" for example) and on cross bars ("f" and "t").

KEY TO COLORS

The colors used for the sampler are given below with the symbols that correspond to the chart for the project. Numbers for DMC six-strand embroidery floss colors are listed in parentheses; other brands are available.

- ☐ lt. blue (519)
- ⊞ med. blue (826)
- + lt. gray (415)
- • white
- ‖ lt. peach (948)
- ✚ peach (353)
- ✕ yellow (973)
- ◪ magenta (718)
- ✤ coral (351)
- ✛ taupe (642)
- ■ navy (311)
- ✦ dark mauve (221)
- ╬ purple (553)
- ♥ mauve (223)
- ▲ med. rust (921)
- ○ silver (001)

MATERIALS AND SUPPLIES

Background. 12" X 18" (30.5cm X 46cm) of No. 14 cross-stitch, even-weave fabric.

Floss. Six-strand embroidery floss in 16 colors, as listed in "Key to Colors."

Needle. Tapestry needle 22 to 26; use the smallest needle you can thread.

Embroidery scissors. the most useful has a small hook on one blade to facilitate removing threads.

and count letter height, width, cross-bar height, stroke widths, serif lengths—all the details that matter in making neat readable lettering. If the letters or designs you want to use are too small to read easily, you can scale them up using another sheet of graph paper. To do this, transfer the lines within each square into larger-size squares, as shown in Fig. 1-10. Making ⅛" (3mm) squares into ¼" (6mm) squares would double the size. ⅛" (3mm) squares into ½" (1.3cm) would make the letters 4 time larger. (Or have them photocopied larger.)

If you want more detail in designing your letters, make large letters on a fine grid. This gives more squares per letter, allowing you to work out the nuances and make smoother shapes. Fig. 1-11 show how this works.

The squares on the grid can correspond to fabric blocks, knit stitches, cross-stitches, or other units of construction. Graphing letters works most easily for block letters (see Fig. 1-13), but it can work for others as well. For more on graphing and designing with letters see Chapter 9.

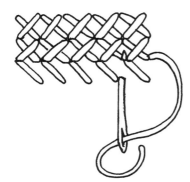

1-14. Cross-stitches are formed using a tapestry (blunt) needle, and all the stitches should cross in the same direction. To make the stitch, sew up through the upper left corner and down through the lower right, making a row with all the stitches in this direction. Then stitch back across the row to cross the stitches—sewing from upper right to lower left.

On a chart graph for a project, the marked squares indicating stitches are either shown in full color or in symbols representing the color. Cross-stitch and needle-point graphs correspond to the number of threads per inch of fabric. This fabric is specially woven so the thread count is even both horizontally and vertically, thus 14 count means 14 stitches per inch.

Cross-Stitching the Project

Before you begin, stay-stitch the edges of the even-weave cross-stitch fabric. Otherwise, since it is loosely woven, it may unravel during handling. Always work with clean hands.

Plan to follow the chart given (see Fig. 1-15 at the end of the chapter), and begin at the top. Enlarge it on a photocopier if you can't see it well enough it. Use a ruler or straightedge to follow the stitch row on the chart. See the "Key to Colors" to determine which color goes in which square of the pattern.

To center the design on the fabric, fold the fabric in half, top to bottom. Then fold it in half again, side to side. This design is 97 squares wide by 131 high. From the center, count 65 squares, which represent rows, to the top of the design and over 48 squares to the left top corner. Mark this point. Begin the blue sky down 7 and in 2 squares.

To cross-stitch, use two strands of the six-strand floss so the stitching won't be too dense. To make the basic cross-stitch, begin each stitch at the bottom left corner of a square and work across the row; then return to make the "X." Reverse this if you are left handed. Be sure all your crossing stitches lie in the same direction, as shown in Fig. 1-14. To make the outline stitch, called "back-stitching," sew a single line of stitches along or across the squares as needed. Develop an even pull on the thread to make firm stitches and yet not so tight they distort the fabric.

Wash and block the design when you are done. The finished design can be stretched on a stiff backing and framed to hang, or sewn into a pillow, clothing, a tote bag, or another object.

2-1. The pieced patchwork shirt in this chapter is easy to make from your favorite fabrics, and the patchwork makes a good background for your favorite saying.

CHAPTER TWO

Sewing Stuff You'll Need

Time to stock your shelves. A project that takes a day to make can take another day to shop for. Friends have joked about all the supplies and tools I've got squirreled away in my studio, but if someone needs a doll needle, purple fabric, Teddy bear eyes, florist's wire, or metallic thread, I've got it! The patchwork-style project in this chapter is assembled from my jumble of fabrics (see Fig. 2-1).

Even so, like any crafts person, I must spend time shopping. One easy way is to read sewing supply catalogs. Okay, I read every catalog no matter what is featured, but I especially like sewing and art supply ones. Not only do they show wonderful products that I must have, but they tell how to use them.

My catalog obsession keeps me in touch with the sewing world. So do magazines such as Robbie Fanning's *Creative Machine, Threads, Fiberarts, American Craft, Sew News,* and quilt magazines. These publications provide good ideas, product information, and recommended craft books. (I confess to a secret delight whenever I come across my own books as I flip the pages.)

Sewing Tools and Supplies

Having good tools and supplies makes sewing much easier and faster. If waiting for mail-ordered treasures takes too long—your inspiration collapses—you can find most of these supplies in a good fabric store. Many of them now carry many craft items as well.

This chapter lists materials you will need to create the projects in the book. Included are sewing tools and supplies, information about fabrics and color choices, and various equipment such as sewing machines. My favorite catalogs are listed in Sources at the end of the book.

Of course you don't need to get everything listed. If your storage space is limited and stores are convenient, let them keep the supplies and buy as needed. Keep only the basic tools on hand. Establish a working place for yourself and keep your tools and supplies nearby in boxes, bags, drawers, or tool kits, whatever works for you.

Cutting Tools

Any cutting tool must be sharp to do a good job, so buy quality tools and keep them in good shape. A sharp tool is a safer tool, too, because you don't have to force it. The precise cuts you get from a sharp tool also means your work turns out better.

Scissors. I think the 7-inch Gingher dressmaker scissors are ideal for general sewing because of their lightweight, yet sharp and sturdy construction. Good-quality, 4-inch embroidery scissors are handy for clipping threads at the sewing machine, cutting out intricate fabric shapes, and sewing by hand. One type of these has a small hook on one blade for picking out threads (see Fig. 2-2). Duck-bill appliqué scissors work well for trimming machine-sewn patches; the duck-bill blade prevents you from cutting the wrong fabric.

Scissors can come in two types, regular ones that shear off the fabric by force, and knife-blade scissors, like the Ginghers, that slice or cut the fabric. You can recognize the knife edge because it has a

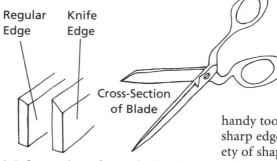

2-3. Some scissors have a knife edge— a more sharply angle blade edge (right cross-section) than regular scissors (left), and are sharper (if cared for).

sharper angle than the regular blades (see Fig. 2-3).

You also will need utility scissors for cutting paper, cardboard, plastic, wire, and all those other things you want to cut. Keep them handy, so you are not tempted to use your fine dressmaker scissors on these materials. It's also important to have your scissors sharpened regularly.

Rotary cutters. These handy tools, which have knife-sharp edges, now come in a variety of shapes and sizes. You will need a cutting mat or other durable surface to place below the fabric you are cutting. Watch your fingers! Use rotary cutters with a

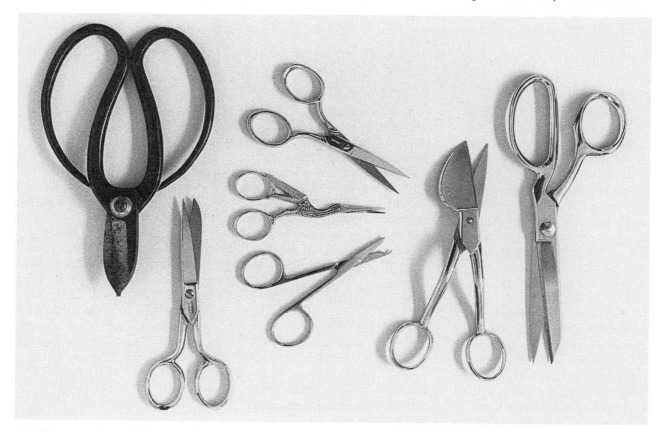

2-2. Keep a variety of scissors on hand for all kinds of alphabet stitchery. Handy types include (left to right) heavy clippers for wires, craft scissors for cutting patterns, three kinds of embroidery scissors, duck-bill appliqué trimmers, and Gingher 7" bent dressmakers (right hand). Note that the bottom pair of embroidery scissors have a small hook to remove threads.

metal ruler for accurate, straight cuts, or cut loosely for random curves. Rotary cutters shear the fabric in place; use razor blades to slit through fabrics such as fake furs or pile fabrics.

Sewing Machines

For most of these projects you will need a machine that is at least new enough to zigzag stitch. If all you have is an old straight-stitch machine, you can still do patchwork, seam joining, and straight-stitch appliqué. You can also do free-motion embroidery with an embroidery foot. Many of the machine-sewn projects in this book could be hand-sewn.

If you have a machine that will zigzag, you can do most of the projects, including the computer-programmed embroidery if you guide your machine by hand with supreme care. But those new computer machines can perform

2-4. *This stuffed Singer sewing machine won't sew a stitch, but it does illustrate a fun way to use lettering in soft sculpture. It was made to commemorate my wedding-present sewing machine, but in fact commemorated my mother's, which I learned on as a child.*

ESSENTIAL PARTS

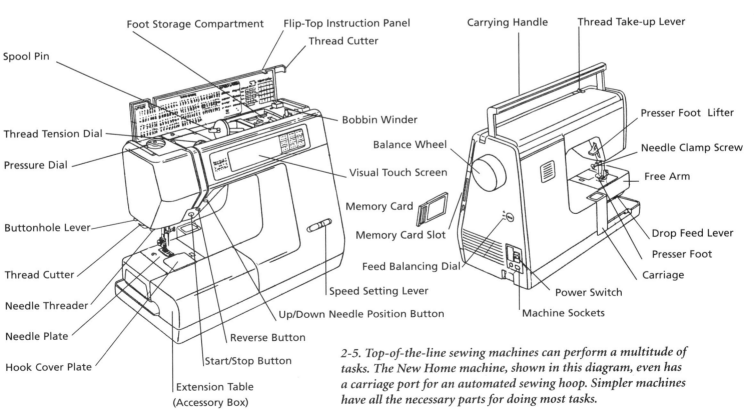

Foot Storage Compartment
Flip-Top Instruction Panel
Thread Cutter
Spool Pin
Thread Tension Dial
Pressure Dial
Buttonhole Lever
Thread Cutter
Needle Threader
Needle Plate
Hook Cover Plate
Bobbin Winder
Balance Wheel
Visual Touch Screen
Memory Card
Memory Card Slot
Feed Balancing Dial
Speed Setting Lever
Up/Down Needle Position Button
Reverse Button
Start/Stop Button
Extension Table (Accessory Box)
Carrying Handle
Thread Take-up Lever
Presser Foot Lifter
Needle Clamp Screw
Free Arm
Drop Feed Lever
Presser Foot
Carriage
Power Switch
Machine Sockets

2-5. *Top-of-the-line sewing machines can perform a multitude of tasks. The New Home machine, shown in this diagram, even has a carriage port for an automated sewing hoop. Simpler machines have all the necessary parts for doing most tasks.*

remarkable feats! See Fig. 2-5 for a diagram of one, and Chapter 5 for details on using them.

Needles

Keep a good supply of needles on hand—both for your sewing machine and for hand sewing—so you can change needles *before* the tip bends or becomes dull. You will also need a variety of needles so you can suit the needle type to the fabric and setting. Needle-Lube, a silicone lubricant, is a good product to have on hand, too. It helps eliminate skipped stitches from friction heat and static electricity.

Other Hand-Sewing Aids

Thimbles. Metal thimbles guard fingers and have indentations you can use to guide and push the needle. Leather thimbles grip the needle to pull, and also have a metal tip to push the needle.

Finger guards. Open plastic finger guards are useful for protecting fingers on either hand as you hand quilt.

Needle grabbers. There are a variety of useful tools you can use to grab and pull uncooperative needles, including leather patches, hemostats, or pliers.

Needle threaders. Use ones with super-fine wire or plastic for hand or machine, regular, or woolly-nylon threads. Some sewing machines have built-in threaders. They are a good idea, but can sometimes be touchy.

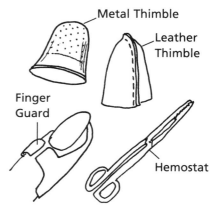

2-6. Thimbles are an essential hand-sewing aid, whether you use traditional metal ones or ones made of soft leather for gripping with a metal tip inside. Finger guards help protect fingers, and hemostats are useful for pulling needles through fabric.

Hoops

A machine embroidery hoop with spring-tension will eliminate wrinkles in solid satin stitching. These hoops are thin enough to slide under the presser foot. Some new computer sewing machines come with automated hoops attached.

Hardwood quilting hoops for hand sewing are adjustable to various thicknesses and come round

---

A GUIDE TO NEEDLE TYPES

Here is a guide to the types of needles you will want to have on hand. Keep in mind that the thickness of sewing machine needles increases as needle size number increases. This is the reverse of hand-sewing needles.

Sewing-Machine Needle Types

Sharps cut through the fibers for the straightest stitch line.

Ballpoints push the fibers aside for a slightly offset stitch line but will not cause runs or holes on knit fabrics.

Topstitching or embroidery needles have a deeper scarf, or thread groove, up the back of the needle to accommodate thicker threads. They also have a longer eye.

Leathers have a wedge cutting point that is useful for piercing leather and plastic.

Twin or doubles make perfect parallel rows on top, a single zigzag row on the back. They are limited to most front-threading zigzag machines.

Hand-Sewing Needle Types

With hand-sewing needles, keep in mind that the higher the number, the shorter the needle. The thickness of hand-sewing needles decreases as size number increases.

Sharps, #11 and #12, are short, (1¼" and 1⅛") thin needles with a small eye for appliqué and quilting.

Betweens, 9# to #12, have a larger eye for easier threading.

Embroidery or crewel needles, sizes #5 to #10 are a favorite general needle with a large long eye for easy threading.

Tapestries, which come in assorted sizes, are blunt needles with a long, easy-to-thread eye. They are used for open mesh materials.

Doll needles are very long, coarse needles (3½" to 5½") used to sew through a thick layer or layers of material.

Glovers or leather needles have a triangular wedge point for piercing without tearing.

---

or oval, up to about 22" (56cm) across. The Q-Snap "Ugly Duckling" frame made of PVC plastic pipe snaps together into a square or rectangle, and "caps" fit over the pipe to hold the quilt in place. For quilting large projects, a full-size quilting frame is useful.

Markers

Many kinds of markers are being used with fabrics, but no one marker can do all you want. For seam lines, you want stability, so the color doesn't bleed into the fabric. In spite of all the new innovations, I still prefer sharp lead pencils or non-water soluble Prismacolor colored pencils for marking the seam lines on the back of fabric. Pencil lines (drawn lightly) can be erased with a gum eraser.

For labels, you want permanency. I use fabric paint on the face of the fabric, since few of the ink markers are really permanent.

For embroidery lines, on the other hand, you want disappearing marks. A tailor's chalk pencil seems to work best for this. You can also mark fabrics with pins, hand basting, or machine-stitching.

Pins and Grippers

Buying 1¼" (3cm) plastic-head quilting pins by the pound might be a good idea, considering the way they seem to disappear. Be sure to get a magnetic pin cushion (one is called Grabbit) to find the pins stuck in the rug or under the sewing machine. I can always tell by the loud yell when my husband has found a pin with his stocking feet. If you are using delicate fabrics, buy fine silk pins.

Chrome safety pins, also bought in bulk, work well for anchoring layers of quilting together. Brass pins may leave marks in the fabric, and straight pins scratch you or fall out in the

sewing. One catalog shows plastic anchors (like clothing tags) put in by a staple gun to baste the quilt together. Stationery-store spring clamps, called bulldog clips, around the edges of a quilt will hold pieces in place for sewing.

Tapes

Masking tape works well to hold fabrics flat for rotary cutting, and then peels off easily. Sewing weights serve the same purpose. Removable Scotch tape is handy for holding buttons, trim, cord, appliqué, or other additions in place for sewing. It sticks on paper patterns as well. Tough silver duct tape is good for taping a quilt top to the floor or table to square it up over the batting. Don't leave any tape in place for an extended period of time, since the adhesive may bond to the fabric.

Threads

These are constructed in various ways to suit different needs. Hand embroidery floss comes in six loose strands; you select the ones you want. Floss colors are listed by code number. Crewel wool yarns are also loosely twisted to maintain the loft of wool, and for better coverage. Hand-sewing thread for quilting is fine and strong, spun or coated with wax to avoid twisting.

Machine sewing thread must be tightly twisted and strong enough to pass up and down through the needle many times before the stitch is formed. Loosely spun threads will shred. Cotton-covered polyester thread provides the color of cotton with the strength of polyester and is the most common general machine sewing thread.

Machine embroidery thread comes in many different fibers for different effects: cotton for bulk, rayon for lustrous color, metallic for glitter, and silk for richness.

These are usually strong enough for the wear and tear of the upper thread position. On the bobbin, you can use heavier, less strong threads for certain effects such as reversed couching (the face side of the fabric is down). To get more thread on the bobbin (winding bobbins is a bore) use a monofilament or fine caliber thread.

Fabrics and Related Supplies

The colors, textures, weights, and types of fabrics change with the seasons. For this reason, many fabric artists keep a big store on hand. (At least that's why they say they keep buying more and more fabrics.) At any rate, it's nice to have many choices on hand when designing a project. Quilters often limit themselves to cotton or cotton-blend (plain-weave) fabrics and store them by colors.

Printed fabrics reflect their times. Quilt historians can date quilts by recognizing styles, materials, and even certain patterns created by specific designers. Some patterns today gain this kind of popularity—the gold celestial designs on navy or the primary-colored cats print are two examples. Ethnic prints from Indonesia and Africa, nature prints, and metallics, in particular, are also popular. Each project in this book recommends suitable fabrics in the supply list for that specific piece.

Fillers and Stuffing

Quilt fabrics are enhanced with padding between layers called filler, batting, or stuffing. It bulks up the outer fabrics and organizes wrinkles into a regular pattern when quilted. Polyester fiberfill, which comes in several weights and types, is most common. Loose for filling toys, it is wispy; bonded, it spreads out like a layer of snow; but bonded and pressed it provides a felted blanket. These days, quilters are using lighter-weight filler with cotton fabrics to make quilting the layers easier and to reduce distortion of their designs. Heavier fabrics may need thicker filler for adequate puffiness.

Fusers and Stabilizers

For easiest appliqué you want to bond one fabric to another. Various products do this. Iron-on fusers hold pieces in place for sewn appliqué; these include Wonder-Under, Stitch-Witchery, and HeatnBond. Ultra Hold HeatnBond will withstand washing without being sewn to secure it. (It may gum up the needle if sewn.) HeatnBond makes a another lighter weight type that is suitable for sewing.

Other bonding agents include glues and sprays, some permanent and some that wash out. Experiment to see what works best on your project. Try them first on a sample piece of fabric. Some will stiffen the fabric, some may change the color. Others may need too much heat to be used with metallics or silks; use low-heat fusers for these materials. If you do not plan to wash your quilt or other project, choose a bonder that won't show or leave marks.

Select the Fabrics

The best way to select fabrics for this shirt is to start with one favorite, and coordinate the others with it. Navy blue predominates in the shirt I made, so the reds all range toward blue—fuchsia, maroon, purple and rust. The yellow is gold (yellow with a little blue and red in it). Colors are

---

PATCHWORK "MAKING-ART" SHIRT

2-7. The letters and words dance across the front of this pieced patchwork shirt. They are fused in place with no sewing needed.

Overview. This easy-to-make shirt design is created by patching together pieces of fabric you may have in your fabric collection. The letters are applied with iron-on adhesive that needs no appliqué stitching.

Technique. I used iron-on cut-out letters. The pieced patchwork fabric shirt is designed for quick construction by serger or sewing machine.

Type style. This project uses Comic Clip, which has letters that are basic block-letter shapes randomly clipped from fabric with sharp scissors. See Fig. 2-8 for the entire alphabet. Use a different type style if you choose.

Size. Amounts given make a medium adult shirt. See "Make and Cut the Pattern" below for directions on creating a pattern in the size you need.

Color concept. Select a group of fabrics that relate in color and character.

dark and muted rather than clear and bright.

The fabrics include ethnic batiks, tiny quilting prints, a Persian rug design print, and solid colors as background for the letters. Fabrics reflect their creation; the batik shows wax-resist designs stamped onto fabric and the rug design reflects the geometry of woven rows. The tiny print in monochrome becomes texture.

Keep the wearer in mind when choosing colors. The right sleeve fabric "washed out" when I tried it next to my face. Choose plain or monochrome fabric for placing the letters, so they don't get lost in the design (unless this strikes your humor for the piece). Make the letters from the same fabrics in related colors. Place light letters on dark fabric, and dark ones on light fabric.

About the Alphabet

The method used to make the letters affects their shape. With cut-out fabric letters you can either aim for perfection by measuring, tracing, and cutting exactly, or you can clip them out in a looser manner. Comic Clip letters reflect the straight line snips and smooth curves made with sharp scissors.

The idea with any typeface is to be consistent. With Comic Clip, the inconsistency of the letter shapes is actually what's consistent, as you can see from Fig. 2-8 (see page 20). When you cut out the letters, as shown in Fig. 2-9 (see page 20), exaggerate the fact that the strokes vary in width, and use the variation as a design element. Note how the strokes widen at the base to give the letters stability. This face is called Comic Clip because you can try funny variations on the letters as you clip. Letters with loops like "**D**," "**R**," and "**O**" are made nearly solid, with only a little round cut-out hole. The "**A**" is consistently inconsistent—each one a little different—and the "**B**" has no holes at all.

Placement of the letters plays an important part in the overall design. They dance across the shirt front instead of marching in straight lines. They clump together in groups, so you know they are words, but their heights vary and they tilt at different angles. The whole thing looks random, but the letters follow a certain rhythm. "Making" swings in on a curve. "Dirty Job" in brown looks uncomfortable and sinks at the end. "Somebody" rises hopefully. The last line (the darkest color) sits solidly weighted down.

MATERIALS AND SUPPLIES

Shirt front fabric. Yokes: two pieces roughly 10" X 11" (25.5cm X 28cm), plus a print strip 3" X 12" (7.5cm X 30.5cm) for the bottom of the left yoke. For the horizontal strips from neck down: Cut one strip off-white 5" X 24" (12.5cm X 61cm); one strip purple-red print 2½" X 24" (6.5cm X 61cm); one peachy-rust triangle 8½" X 24" (22cm X 61cm); one batik strip 2½" X 24" (53.5cm X 61cm); one strip maroon print 5" X 24" (12.5cm X 61cm); and a double bottom strip 6" X 24" (15cm X 61cm).

Shirt back. Repeat front, except cut the yoke in one piece, and cut yoke lining or vary the patch pattern depending on fabrics on hand.

Sleeves. Two pieces 21" X 14" (53.5cm X 3.5cm); two cuffs 11" X 6" (28cm X 15cm).

Recommended fabrics. Cotton and cotton-poly blend fabrics are preferred. Use firmly woven, non-fraying fabrics.

Tools and supplies. Interfacing, ruler, large pieces of paper (unprinted newsprint, shelf paper, wrapping paper), pencil, tape measure, sharp embroidery scissors, a serger or sewing machine, threads, an iron, and an ultra-hold, iron-on adhesive like HeatnBond that does not need topstitching to remain in place.

PICK A SAYING

Let your clothing carry your thoughts. Those talking heads on TV aren't the only ones expressing themselves in public. Anybody can do it these days via T-shirts and decorated clothing.

Don't be limited by the saying I picked for this project. You can find sayings to use everywhere—*Bartlett's Quotations*, Shakespeare, TV, or a friend's bulletin board, to name a few. You've probably got an old family favorite. My dad always said, "The harder I work, the luckier I get." Mary Zee says, "Time is too valuable to spend it all working." How about; "We are what we save"? And then there are lots of in-your-face messages on shirts walking around out there.

2-8. Comic Clip Alphabet . This is a block-style alphabet that reflects the way it's made—the letters are clipped with scissors. Note how the strokes broaden at the base for stability and vary in width to give a hand-made playful appearance.

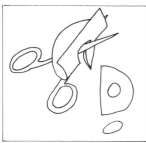

2-9. To clip out letters with holes, like "D" or "O," fold the letter in half and clip out the center.

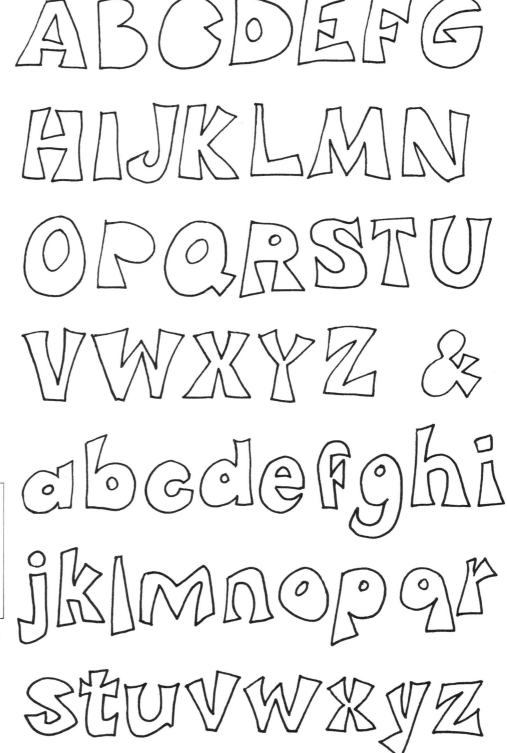

Make and Cut the Pattern

To adjust the size of the pattern, measure the chest and hips of the person you are making it for. Add about 4" (10cm) of ease to the measurement across the shirt front. Scale the whole pattern up to this dimension. Measure the scaled-up cuff size, and compare it with the size of the person's arm halfway up from the wrist. If the scaled-up cuff isn't large enough, draw it the right size, adding 2" (5cm) of ease, and draw the angle of the sleeve to meet it.

1. Draw a full-sized pattern on paper. Make the pieces shown in Fig. 2-10: full-sized shirt front and back, shirt front yokes, back yoke, sleeves, and cuff.

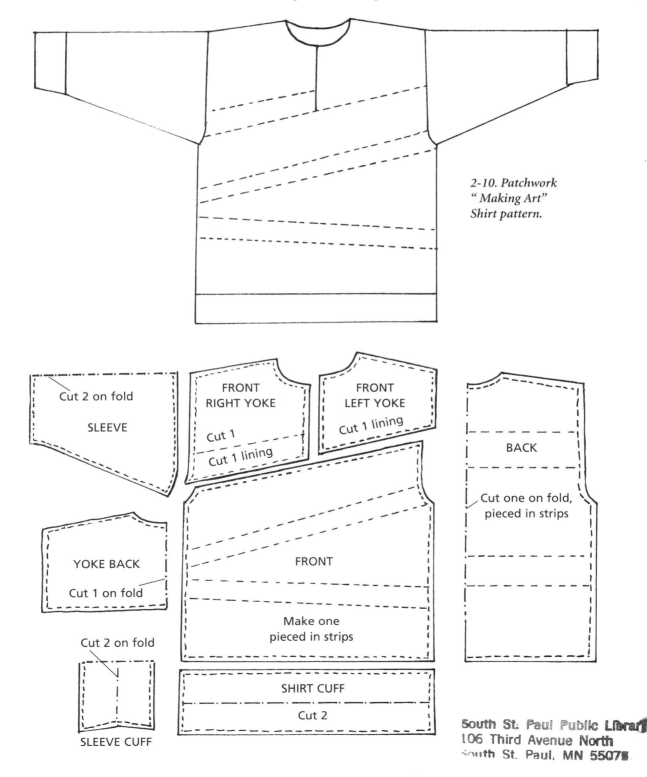

2-10. Patchwork " Making Art" Shirt pattern.

Cut 2 on fold

SLEEVE

FRONT RIGHT YOKE

Cut 1

Cut 1 lining

FRONT LEFT YOKE

Cut 1 lining

BACK

Cut one on fold, pieced in strips

YOKE BACK

Cut 1 on fold

FRONT

Make one pieced in strips

Cut 2 on fold

SHIRT CUFF

Cut 2

SLEEVE CUFF

2. Make a second paper pattern of the shirt front. Draw seam lines for the pieced fabric strips on the shirt front according to the pattern shown, or design your own patch pattern. To design your own, sketch where you want the words to appear on the shirt first. Don't position them too near the edges, or they will be lost on the sides of the shirt when it is worn. Try on the lettered paper pattern to see how your design works. (Be sure a seam appears across the base of the front neck opening.)

3. Try various fabrics to choose colors and placements before cutting: fold fabrics to size and place them on the pattern to see how they blend. Keep changing them around until you get a design you like.

4. Once you are satisfied with fabrics, cut the shirt-front pattern into strips. Then cut out the fabric pieces; be sure to add ½" (2.5cm) seam allowances all around each piece. Cut interfacing for the yokes if needed.

For me this wasn't a neat process. I folded and tried fabrics, serged and removed seams, pressed and pinned parts. My heap of possible fabrics grew tall by the time I'd made all my choices. You need to keep a stock on hand for this technique.

Assemble the Shirt Front

This shirt is designed to be made quickly by serger or sewing machine. This means uncomplicated seams. Cuffs and hem are folded and serged on to complete the shirt with no hand sewing or hems to turn.

1. Piece the shirt front strips together, and join the strip to the two sides of the yoke (see Fig. 2-11).

2. Align the shirt front yoke with its lining, face-to-face (see Fig. 2-12). Add interfacing if

Front Left Yoke　　Front Right Yoke

FRONT

2-11

needed. Seam the neck opening and neck curve. Trim the seam allowance, turn, and press. Repeat for the other side. Align and tape the yokes together.

3. Match completed yokes with the shirt front and serge or overcast-stitch across the front. Remove the tape and press the seam downward. Lay the assembled front on the full-sized pattern to check for accuracy. Redo any seams that skew the shirt from the pattern.

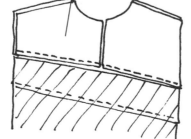

Lining and Yoke, face-to-face

Sew neck opening and turn

2-12

Add the Letters

1. Draw your wording on the plain paper pattern shirt front. Placement may change, but this will give you letter sizes. Flip the pattern over, and trace the letters on the reverse side (they will be reversed).

2. Select the fabrics for each word or phrase.

3. Cut the HeatnBond into strips the height of the words, probably about 1¼" (3cm) to 2" (5cm). Lay the adhesive strips with the paper backing side *up* on the reversed wording. (A light box or lighted window helps for this.) Trace or sketch the letters close together on the strip, ignoring pattern placement. Iron the adhesive strips on the right color of fabric.

4. Using sharp embroidery scissors, clip out the letters (see Fig. 2-13). Make long clips instead of sawing the scissors. Clip from the edge to the center rather than turning corners. For closed letters ("**A**," "**D**," "**R**") fold the letter over the opening and clip. Peel off the backing paper.

5. Lay the shirt front on the ironing board, or flat surface. Arrange the letters according to

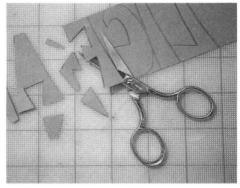

2-13. To make your saying, draw letters in reverse on fusible backing (don't leave spacing between letters). Then iron it on the back of the fabric and clip out the letters to be ironed onto the shirt.

the pattern or shift them until you like the layout. Place each exactly as you want it and press in place. Don't move the iron as you press.

Assemble the Shirt

1. Assemble the shirt back strips, except for the yoke lining. Match the shirt front and back at the shoulders, face-to-face (see Fig. 2-14). Note that the unseamed back shoulder is wider at the neck.

Match at shoulders

2-14

2. Lay the back yoke lining face-to-face with the front yoke (see Fig. 2-15). Sew the shoulder seams and sew the back neck seam exactly next to the front neck seam. Trim and align the back yoke with the back. Neck and shoulder raw edges are now concealed.

3. Align the sleeve face-to-face with the arm hole (see Fig. 2-16). Sew the sleeve to the shirt by serger or overcast, and repeat for the other sleeve.

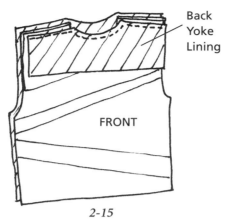

Back Yoke Lining

FRONT

2-15

4. Align and sew the shirt and sleeve side seams.

5. To finish the sleeves, fold the sleeve cuff to align the side edges and sew into a tube. Trim, turn, and fold, so the cuff is a doubled tube. Align the raw edges and press the fold. Then tuck the cuff into the sleeve, align the raw edges, and sew or serge (see Fig. 2-17). Repeat for the other cuff.

6. To finish the bottom seam, fold the shirt cuff to align the side edges, and sew into a tube. Trim, turn, and fold so the cuff is dou-

bled. Align the raw edges and press the fold. Align the raw edges face-to-face with the shirt and sew or serge.

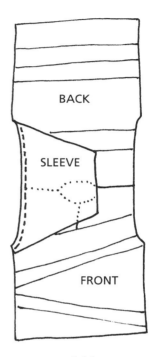

BACK

SLEEVE

FRONT

2-16

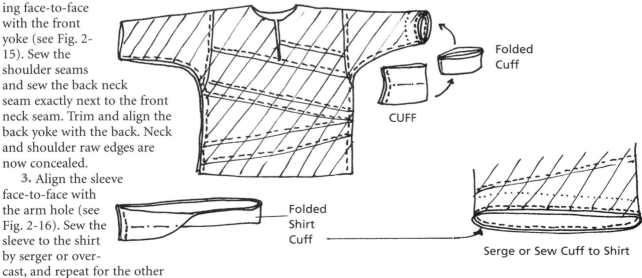

Folded Cuff

CUFF

Folded Shirt Cuff

Serge or Sew Cuff to Shirt

2-17

23

3-1. *This chapter's project, the ABC Animal Quilt, requires accuracy in appliqué and topstitching, but it's worth the effort.* Photo by Laurie Tennant.

CHAPTER THREE

ABC Quilts

ABC quilts are not only educational for children, they are a delightful way to become familiar with letters. Learning the ABCs is a first step every child takes toward reading. They learn that alphabet letters are the basic units of words, visual symbols of sounds.

Our alphabet provides 26 different letters to make into a quilt design. The letter can vary enormously in shape depending on the design of the quilt. The letters can be made as solid, simple blocks or as large shapes filled with complex designs, as in Mary Zee's quilt, a detail of which appears in Fig. 3-2. (See Fig. 9-4 for the entire quilt.) Letters also can feature a refined typeface commonly used in storybooks, such as the roman face used for the *ABC Animal Quilt*, the project for this chapter, shown in Fig. 3-1. All the type styles shown in this book and a hundred more are yours to choose from in designing your own quilt.

One common form for ABC quilts is a grid of blocks separated by sashing, with the letters appliquéd, embroidered, or knitted onto the blocks. Grid block quilts are the focus of this chapter. Other arrangements are possible, such as the *ABC Objects Quilt* in Chapter 10, which has a free-form design.

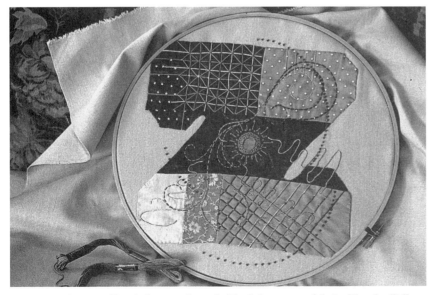

3-2. Mary Zee appliqués fat, patchwork, block letters on fabric, like the "Z" shown here. She then puts them in an embroidery hoop to embellish with stitching and beading.

Designing ABC Quilts

Most of us approach the design of an alphabet quilt backwards—we begin with the letters. This is logical, since letters are the main idea, but it presents problems: it is hard to fit all the letters into a quilt design. That's because 26 is not an easy number to divide into a grid for a quilt. Inevitably, you have to add additional blocks, combine letters on a block, or cope in some other creative manner.

Since the design considerations listed below all affect each other, you will need to consider them all together. In one order or another, you need to develop a theme, select the letter style, design the block, plan the overall layout, make a pattern, and decide on sewing technique.

For example, if you begin by deciding on quilt size first, you would divide that space into a grid of blocks for letters. Or you can design a block size you like and see what size quilt this would turn out to be. Children's quilts can range from baby quilts as small as a yard (.9m) square to single bed size. If you plan to use the quilt as a wall hanging, don't make it larger than 60" X 72" (1.52m X 1.83m). Either way you plan to begin, it's best to start doodling on paper to try out your ideas.

Choose a Theme

Some theme is always apparent on ABC quilts, whether it be straight-forward lettering, lively colors, appealing fabrics, interesting arrangement, or added embellishments. Sometimes the letters themselves are the theme, either as simple shapes or complex ones, like the ones shown in Fig. 3-3.

It's fun and challenging to choose a theme such as flowers, foods, or toys, and then find an example for every letter. On the *ABC Animal Quilt* for this chapter, the greatest challenge was finding the "X." I used *Xiphosura,* the scientific name for horseshoe crab (see Fig 3-4). As for "U," you might quibble that the Unicorn is

3-3. Start with a theme to design your own letters and quilt squares for an ABC quilt. Try designing fat appliquéd letters, cat-shaped ones, square-shaped letters on print fabric, embroidered flower letters, or any other ideas you have.

3-4. What do you choose for an "X" square on an ABC animal quilt? It took a bit of research, but the scientific name for a horseshoe crab is Xiphosura.

an imaginary animal, but the South American Umbrella Bird could substitute. Encyclopedias obviously come in handy.

Fortunately for us, the English alphabet has only 26 letters, while the Cyrillic or Russian alphabet has 35 and the Japanese has thousands of *congi,* or characters. What a challenge a Japanese alphabet quilt would be!

Select Type Style and Design the Block

In designing your own quilt, the type style you choose will have

ABCDEFG
HIJKLMN
OPQRSTU
VWXYZ &
abcdefghi
jklmnopqr
stuvwxyz

3-5. Palatino Alphabet. You can trace, enlarge, or use this page of roman type as a drawing guide.

visual weight determined by the width of its lines and the darkness of the color used. You can select one of the type styles in this book or experiment with designing your own. For the *ABC Animal Quilt*, I used letters based on a typeface called Palatino, shown in Fig. 3-5 (page 27), and adapted them somewhat to fit my design. The patterns for the quilt blocks, Fig. 3-21 on pages 37 to 41, shows my adaptation of the letters.

To test your type, draw a letter on paper or cut it out of colored paper, then combine it with the theme imagery to see how it looks. Simple drafting tools and supplies are all you'll need: a T-square, tracing paper, pencil, circle guides, scale ruler, etc. (See "Making and Using Letters" in Chapter 1 for information on these supplies.) Use a pad of graph paper for sketching. Ignore the lines at first to keep loose in your sketching. Often your first sketches are the liveliest. Then use the graph to refine the sketch, measure proportion, and scale up your design. Work in erasable pencil; then draw in the main lines in ink when you've decided which they are.

It will look best to make all your letters the same general size, at least in height, if you plan to combine them with imagery. Try various arrangements, perhaps with the letter centered, overlapping the imagery, or with the letter toward the upper left corner and a cluster of images below right. Draw different kinds of designs—animals carrying letters, little carts of flowers, people-shaped letters, or letters as design objects themselves. Then, once you get a design idea, carry it out in some consistent form for every letter. A quilt would probably look too disjointed if you made each letter block entirely different.

(Well, maybe not. You could give yourself the challenge to try it.)

Plan the Overall Grid

Once you have the letters and any related artwork designed to your satisfaction, consider the whole quilt. For formal harmony, design each block alike, placing the letter in the same position on each square. The more hand-drawn your letters appear, and the further they depart from traditionally accurate letters, the looser you can be with placement. At this stage, try different placements to see what looks best to you. Let the ideas in Fig. 3-6 help get you started.

Make small sketches of your quilt plan on graph paper to measure the border, sashings, and center. What size and shape do you plan? Decide on the number of blocks, their shape, and their size, which all affect the shape and size of the quilt.

The *ABC Animal Quilt* has 30 blocks, with four "extra" blocks appearing in the corners. The "extra" blocks have simple appliqué designs representing the heavens (sky), the water (waves), the earth (mountains), and plants (a tree). Mary's Zee's quilt (see Fig. 9-5, on page 103) has 28 horizontal blocks that are arranged 4 blocks across by 7 blocks down. The two extra blocks tell about the quilt makers and owners.

You can make a quilt with 24 blocks (4 x 6 blocks) if you combine a few thin letters—"I" with "J" and "S" with "T," perhaps. A 36-block quilt (6 x 6) could include the numbers from 0 to 9. Extra blocks could be filled with punctuation marks—an exclamation point (!), ampersand (&), question mark (?), or math symbols (+,–, X). If you have selected a theme like flowers, food, toys, or clowns, fill in with related design symbols.

Once you have determined the number and shape of the blocks, lay the grid out on graph paper to determine the size of sashings and borders. This can also serve as your fabric-amount guide. Don't forget to figure in seam allowances on all pieces.

Make the Patterns

The next step is to scale the letters up to size. Unless you enlarged them on a photocopier, you probably have to neaten them to make the pattern. Letters must be shaped accurately to look right. If you are using a different set of letters from mine, measure them for design consistencies, and draw an accurate pattern. With the roman typeface used on the *Animal ABC Quilt*, the heavy strokes are all essentially the same width; the light strokes are as well. Note which strokes are heavy and which light (see Fig. 3-7 as a guide). The round letters will be ovals. Measure the width of the serifs (stroke endings) and note how they join to the stroke.

Use a guide with top and bottom lines for height to draw your letters (see Fig. 1-9, on page 7). Block letter strokes are all the same width, except for a few instances in lowercase letters or numbers. Some capital letters will go above the top line and below the bottom line in formal typefaces. This is because round letters (including "C," "G," "O," "Q," and "S") need to be taller to appear to be the same volume as the boxier letters. Sometimes the swash on the "R" and "K" go below the line.

In casual lettering you need not be as exact, but the letters must all be consistent—consistently casual, consistently fat, wavy, loopy, tall, whatever. Combine the design theme with

24-BLOCK GRID

A	B	C	D
E	F	G	H
IJ	K	L	M
N	O	P	Q
R	S	T	UV
W	X	Y	Z

30-BLOCK GRID

🌳	A	B	C	☁
D	E	F	G	H
I	J	K	L	M
N	O	P	Q	R
S	T	U	V	W
≈	X	Y	Z	𝕸

36-BLOCK GRID

A	B	C	D	E	F
G	H	I	J	K	L
M	N	O	P	Q	R
S	T	U	V	W	X
Y	Z	0	1	2	3
4	5	6	7	8	9

BABY BLOCK QUILT

28-BLOCK GRID

A	B	C	≋
D	E	F	G
H	I	J	K
L	M	N	O
P	Q	R	S
T	U	V	W
▦	X	Y	Z

BABY BLOCKS PATTERN

3-6. ABC quilt grids can be designed with varying numbers of blocks, including 24, 28, 30, and 36. Or make an optical illusion baby block quilt.

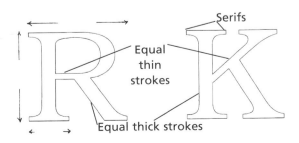

3-7. Unlike block letters, which have strokes that are all the same width, roman letters always have thick and thin strokes. In a single alphabet, the thick and thin strokes are of consistent width. They nearly always have serifs, or wider finishing strokes.

your letter pattern onto the block, then make a full-size drawing. This will be your pattern.

Design for Appliqué

Appliqué is a French word meaning to apply a fabric motif to a background fabric by sewing. Because fabrics are flexible and woven, the motif pieces should be designed large enough to handle readily and firm enough to maintain their shapes without fraying or pulling out of shape.

In traditional appliqué, motif pieces are cut with a narrow hem around the edges that is then turned under. The piece is held down with hidden stitching along the edges, or an exposed line of buttonhole stitching. This stitch looks like a row of joined right angles (see Fig. 3-8). Hand-sewn appliqué pieces have a charming puffiness caused by the hem.

The invention of fusible webbing—and the sewing machine—make appliqué easier and faster. Now you can trace the letter (in reverse) on the paper backing of the fusible webbing, iron the fuser on the back of the motif fabric, cut out the letter, remove the paper, place the letter on the background fabric, and iron it in place. Use a sewing machine to satin-stitch the motif firmly in place; no puff, no wrinkles.

Even so, the nature of fabric must be taken into account in designing letter shapes to be fused. I keep mentioning this because the roman letters I used push the limits. They are long and narrow, and tend to shift even with fused adhesive on the backs. For the sake of accuracy, these letters were appliquéd using a stacking technique.

You will find complete directions for using the stacking technique in the instructions for the *ABC Animal Quilt*. It involves placing a paper pattern, the motif fabric, and the background fabric in a stack, pinning or taping them in place, and then sewing the outlines of the motif right through the entire stack of paper and fabrics. Once the pattern is torn away, then the motif edges are trimmed close to the stitch line, and then the raw edge satin stitched by machine.

Machine satin-stitching not only holds the motif in place, it becomes a strong outline element in the design. If the thread chosen matches the motif, the satin-stitch outline will not stand out. If the thread contrasts with the motif, it will. All the satin-stitch outlining on the *ABC Animal Quilt* is done in black to look like early children's book illustrations.

You can use either method in making the project quilt. If you plan to fuse on the letters, use a light box to place the letters accurately. Lay the motif with fused backing (paper removed) on the fabric block over the paper design pattern. Align the cut-out fused letter with the pattern outline and tape in place with masking or

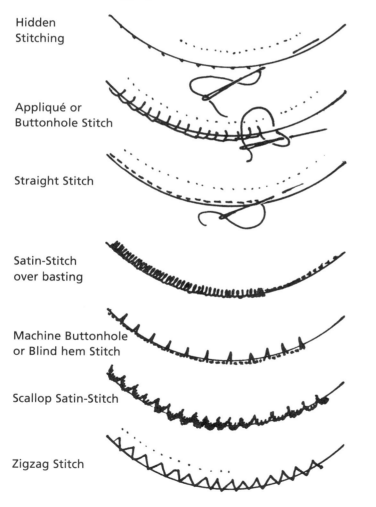

Hidden Stitching

Appliqué or Buttonhole Stitch

Straight Stitch

Satin-Stitch over basting

Machine Buttonhole or Blind hem Stitch

Scallop Satin-Stitch

Zigzag Stitch

3-8. There are several types of appliqué stitching. The top three shown here are hand stitches, while the bottom four are machine stitches.

removable tape. Move it to the ironing board carefully so nothing shifts and press it in place. Press the iron down straight, then lift and move it, rather than push it back and forth. Don't iron over the tape.

There's always something. Machine satin-stitching has a major tendency to pucker or stretch fabric even when sewn with a fused backing. The machine's take-up lever in combination with the bobbin case retards the threads in order to form and balance the stitch. This tension on every stitch pulls in the base fabric as well. A really solid row of satin-stitching can stretch both fabrics and buckle up into a bumpy outline.

Both instances require a fabric stabilizer of some kind. A sewing machine hoop helps, but even with one, you need a stiff backing. Plain typing paper on the back works as a removable stabilizer. The stitch line perforates it, so it tears off readily. The paper pattern laid over the motif also can serve to stabilize if you remove only the paper outside the motif. Satin-stitch the outline and tear off the paper, removing any tiny bits with tweezers. Tear-away stabilizers that leave no paper bits behind are available in fabric stores. Or you can permanently sew in a firmly woven fabric backing.

More specific details on appliqué, pattern and template making, piecing the quilt, and assembling it appear in the following project instructions.

Making Patterns and Templates

For the pattern for the quilt blocks see Fig. 3-21; for the sashing pattern, see Fig. 3-20. Both are at the end of this chapter.

ABC ANIMAL QUILT

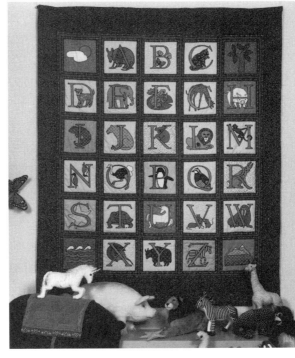

Overview. This wall-hung or bed quilt has appliquéd animals and letters on each block. Stripe-patterned sashing fabric is mitered at the corners to frame the blocks. The theme features an animal for every letter of the alphabet.

Technique. Detailed instructions for two special techniques are given: stacked appliqué and mitered corners. In stacked appliqué, fabrics are stacked behind the pattern paper (or a copy), which acts as the stitching guide. Excess fabric is trimmed off after stitching. I didn't use iron-on fusers for this quilt, because accuracy is vital; even the movement of the iron tends to shift fusible letters out of true. If you have a press you can fuse the pieces.

Type style. The typeface used is similar to Palatino, but I adapted the letters a bit when I created the quilt. You will find the letters I used in the pattern for the quilt Fig. 3-21. There are a variety of other roman typefaces that would work well for an alphabet quilt, such as Goudy Old Style (pronounced GOW-dee).

Size: 58½" X 71" (149cm X 179cm). Individual blocks are 7½" (19cm) square. Sashing is 2" (5cm) wide, side border is 4½" (12cm), top and bottom borders are 6" (15cm).

Color concept. The main tones of the quilt are warm pastels on light backgrounds, outlined in black and framed with a dark print. Animals done in plain colors were put on printed backgrounds, animals in printed fabrics are on plain backgrounds, white animals and scenes are on darker backgrounds. None of the colors are clear primaries (red, yellow, blue) and only black and white are used full intensity. So many colors are used it is unlikely you will find them all. Just assemble all the colors you can, and then relate new ones to this group. Don't worry if some aren't perfect, as long as they all harmonize. See Color Fig. C-2 for a color photograph of the quilt.

1. Enlarge each block pattern to 7½" (19cm) square on white copy paper or tracing paper. Make one-sided copies, with no lines on the back to show through. If you make your blocks larger or smaller, alter other quilt dimensions and fabric amounts to match. NOTE: The stacking technique ruins the pattern by stitching through it as a guide, so make two copies and retain one.

2. Make cardboard templates for the sashing pattern pieces. Cut separate templates, as shown in Fig. 3-20, for A-1 (reversed, this template becomes A-2), B and C.

3. Make a template out of a 10½" (27cm) square piece of matt board with an opening 7½" (19cm) square. Use an X-acto knife and T-square guide for accuracy. Or use four strips of matt board, 10½" X 1½" (27cm X 4cm) to tape together the square, using a right-angle triangle for accuracy on the inside corners. You will use this template to lightly trace seam lines on the back of each completed block.

Cutting Technique for Stacked Appliqué

1. Cut out the fabric background squares. Pieces are 8½" (22cm) square for ½" (1.3cm) seam allowances, or 9½" (24.3cm) for 1" (2.5cm) seam allowances, which I prefer.

2. Assemble the fabrics needed for animal and letter pattern pieces.

3. To make the "A" block, cut a blue fabric piece that is ½" (13mm) larger (more or less) than the "A" letter, about 7" (18cm) square. Accuracy is not important yet, only that the fabric entirely cover the pattern, and that the grain of the fabric runs true. (The size of the piece you will need will vary from letter to letter.) Cut a gold-colored piece

for the armadillo, 7" (18cm) square.

4. To begin assembling the stack, tape the pattern face down on the light box or window so you can see the pattern lines clearly. Place the blue "A" appliqué fabric face down on the back of the pattern (see Fig. 3-9). Adjust it so it covers the "A" (visible through the paper) completely. Tape or pin it in place on the paper pattern.

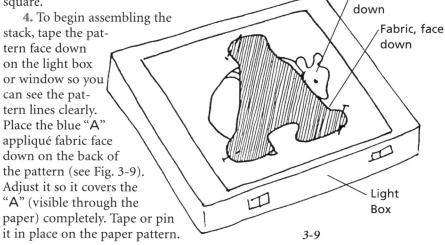

3-9

MATERIALS AND SUPPLIES

Background fabric. You will need a total of 2¼ yards (206cm) in eight different colors: 12 pieces cream, 6 pieces cream pink print, 3 pieces medium blue dot, 1 pieces plain blue, 2 pieces blue/white print, 2 pieces green print, 2 pieces tan stripe, 2 pieces tiny print on white.

Animal appliqué fabric. Select mixed patterns related to animal colors—gold, tan gray, white, brown, black/white stripe, etc.

Letter appliqué fabric. Pink ½ yard (46cm), blue ½ yard (46cm).

Sashing fabric. 1½ yards (137cm) of 44" (111cm) wide striped "ribbon pattern."

Backing fabric. 60" X 72" (152cm X 183cm), buy 4 yards (3.65 meters) of fabric.

Recommended fabrics. Use tightly woven poly-cotton or cotton fabrics to avoid fraying. For the letters, choose pink and blue drapery-weight fabric, so the overlapped fabrics behind will not shadow through. You may wish to wait until you have finished all the squares to choose a print sashing fabric, but if you have found the perfect sashing fabric, relate your colors to it.

Filler. Bonded batt or fiberfill, 5 feet X 6 feet (152cm X183cm).

Thread. Black machine embroidery thread for outlining satin-stitch.

Tools and supplies. Light box, T-square, embroidery or appliqué scissors, iron, tape, pins, matt board (for frame and templates), backing, typing paper, X-acto knife, and a right angle triangle guide to check miters.

Place pins outside any stitch lines, since a pin hidden in this sandwich and sewn over is hard on your sewing machine—and hard on you if you get stuck.

5. Place the gold fabric face down on the blue fabric and pattern, then adjust so it covers the armadillo pattern lines completely (see Fig. 3-10). Tape or pin in place. Lay the block fabric face down on the stack of gold fabric, blue fabric, and the pattern. Adjust the pattern edges with the block-edge seam line so the grain is true. Tape or pin in the corners, out of the way of stitch lines.

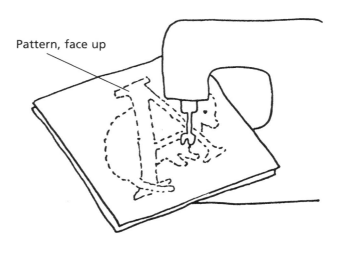

Pattern, face up

3-11

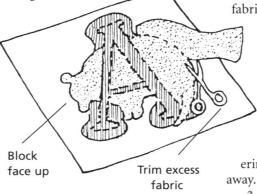

Gold Armadillo fabric face down

All pins outside stitch lines

3-10

Basting and Trimming the Appliqué:

1. Set your sewing machine to a very short stitch length, or a short, narrow zigzag stitch. Use a light-colored or black thread, which will be covered and not show once the block is finished.

2. Slide the pattern/fabric sandwich with the pattern face up under your presser foot (see Fig. 3-11). Stitch all the lines of the pattern through the paper, including detail lines within the appliqué piece such as the armadillo's eye and plate divi-

sions. Where the armadillo tail overlaps the foot of the "A," follow the tail, not the lines of the "A."

3. Remove pins or tape from the stitch-perforated pattern piece, and tear it away from the stitch lines.

4. Using appliqué scissors (with a duck-bill lower blade) or sharp embroidery scissors, trim away the seam allowance around the "A." Take *extreme* care not to cut the background fabric. (That's what the appliqué scissors are designed

Block face up

Trim excess fabric

3-12

for, to save you from this trauma.) The finished seam allowance should be as narrow as possible.

5. Next, trim away the gold fabric outside the stitch lines (see Fig. 3-12). Do not trim the stitch lines that show body details. Do trim on either side of the armadillo's tail where it crosses the "A." Handle the block with care so the closely trimmed appliqué pieces do not pull out.

Outline with Satin-Stitch

1. Thread your machine with black embroidery thread and set the stitch width for about 1/8" (3mm to 4mm), or as needed to cover the stitched line holding the appliqué piece in place.

2. Add stabilizer behind the fabric block during satin-stitching. Either use a permanent backing like a firm fabric covering the entire piece, or use a removable backing such as typing paper or tear-away stabilizer. The stabilizer remains under the satin-stitched line to keep it from puckering after the extra is torn away.

3. Satin-stitch around the letter "A," keeping the stitch lines

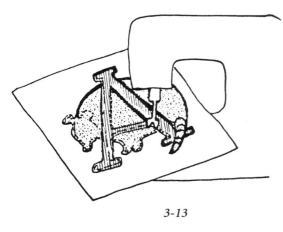

3-13

crisp and straight (see Fig. 3-13). This black outline increases the width of the letter outlines and the armadillo outline, so keep the form of the animal in mind as you stitch.

4. Set the machine to narrower satin-stitch for the body details. This line need not be as wide as stitches holding the appliqué pieces in place.

5. Repeat Steps 3 to 5 under "Cutting Technique for Stacked Appliqué," then baste, trim, and outline stitch the appliqué pattern for each block in the quilt.

Assembling the Quilt with Mitered Corners

1. The next step is to cut out the sashing and the border pieces. On the back of the fabric, align the sashing template with the striped lines of the fabric to make sure the print matches at the corners. Trace seam lines with black or white pencil. Add ½" (1.3cm) seam allowances around each piece, then cut out the pieces listed on Fig. 3-20. Be sure to leave space for ½" (13cm) seam allowances around every piece.

2. To sew the sashing and blocks together, you need to draw seam lines on the back of each block. To do this, tape the second copy of the pattern face down on the light box. Place the appliquéd block face down over it, and align the block with the pattern. Tape it down, if necessary. Lay the frame template you made over this, then trace the seam line (see Fig. 3-14). To avoid puckers in the fabric pull your pencil toward you. If the satin-stitching pulled in the fabric, use a contrasting-color Prisma-color pencil, which won't bleed, to

redraw inaccurate seam lines. Be accurate.

3. Now, begin to assemble the quilt face. Pin an A-1 sashing piece to the left side of the cloud block, face-to-face. Align the seam lines, insert pins at each end and along the seam line. Then stitch this seam by hand or machine, removing pins as you stitch (see Fig. 3-15).

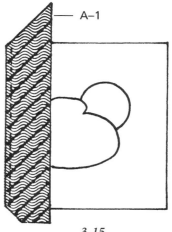

3-15

4. Align and pin the A-2 sashing piece to the top edge of the block, as above. Sew this seam,

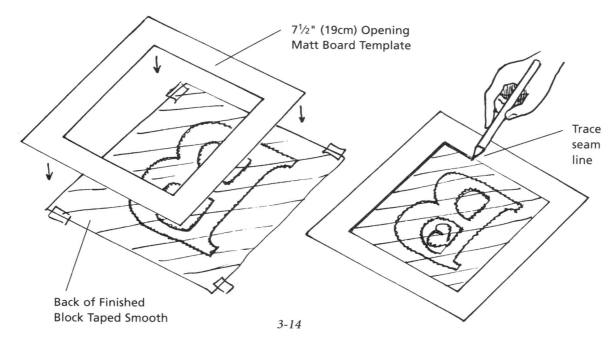

7½" (19cm) Opening
Matt Board Template

Trace seam line

Back of Finished Block Taped Smooth

3-14

stopping at the corner to adjust the fabrics for the mitered corner (see Fig. 3-16). At the corner, pivot the sashing to align and pin the prints; stitch the short angle. If the corner isn't accurate, check the seam lines with a 45-degree triangle and resew.

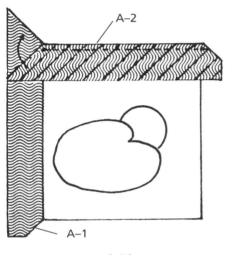

3-16

5. Pin a C sashing to the right side of the cloud block, and sew to the corner (see Fig. 3-17). Pivot as above and sew the seam. Then pin the same C sashing to the left side of the armadillo block and stitch. Pivot at the block corner to stitch. Pin a B sashing to the top edge of the armadillo block and

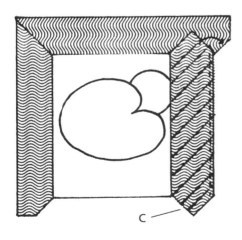

3-17

stitch. Pivot twice to sew the angles of the mitered corner. Sew the C sashing to the left side of the butterfly block, and sew a B sashing to the top. Continue across the row.

6. Complete the row by sewing an A-1 sashing on top of the tree block and an A-2 on the right side. Press the seams flat together toward the sashing so they will not shadow the blocks.

7. Assemble the next four rows of blocks, using B and C sashings as shown. As you assemble, consult Fig. 3-18 to get the sashing pieces placed correctly.

8. Assemble the bottom row, using A-1, A-2 pieces at the ends, C sashing between the blocks, and B sashing across the bottom (see Fig. 3-19).

9. Lay the "ABC" row face-to-face with the "D" to "H" row. Align and pin

the seams. Depending on your skill you may wish to machine sew this row across the blocks and go back to sew the mitered corners. This allows you to check them for accuracy. Even though seam lines are traced accurately on the back,

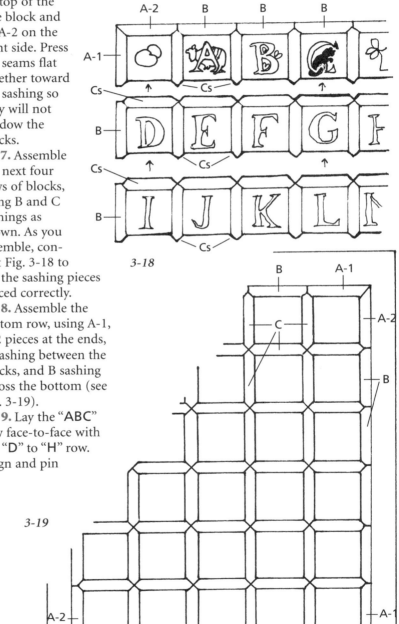

3-18

3-19

fabric shifts and you may need to adjust the miters for accuracy. Complete sewing the rows together in this manner. Press the seams flat toward the sashing.

10. Measure and mark the seam lines on the border fabrics. Pin them on and stitch. Press.

Assembling the Quilt Layers

1. To make the backing, cut two pieces of backing fabric 30" X 72" (76cm X 183cm). Sew them together lengthwise to make a piece 60" X 72" (152cm X 183cm). Press this seam open.

2. Make a sandwich of the bonded batting, the face-up quilt, and the face-down backing. To do this, spread out the batting on the floor or large table. Lay the quilt top face-side-up on the filler (batting), smooth it flat and square it. If necessary use pins or tape to secure the quilt face to a flat surface and check the sides for even lengths and the corners for square. Lay the backing on the quilt face down. Align the edges, trim the batting and backing to size and pin or secure the edges.

3. Untape the quilt face. Machine sew around the layers, leaving an 18" (46cm) opening to turn. Trim the edges, cutting the filler

off at the seam, clip across the corners, and turn.

4. Press the edges, sew the opening shut, and pin or baste around the quilt edge to secure the edge seam.

5. Lay the quilt flat, smooth and square it, then secure it to the table or floor with tape or pins. Safety pin or otherwise baste the layers together at 6" (15cm) intervals. Untape the quilt.

6. Machine stitch in the ditch or hand quilt on the sashing edges. If the quilt sags or will be used and washed, hand or machine quilt around the appliqué shapes within the blocks for added stability.

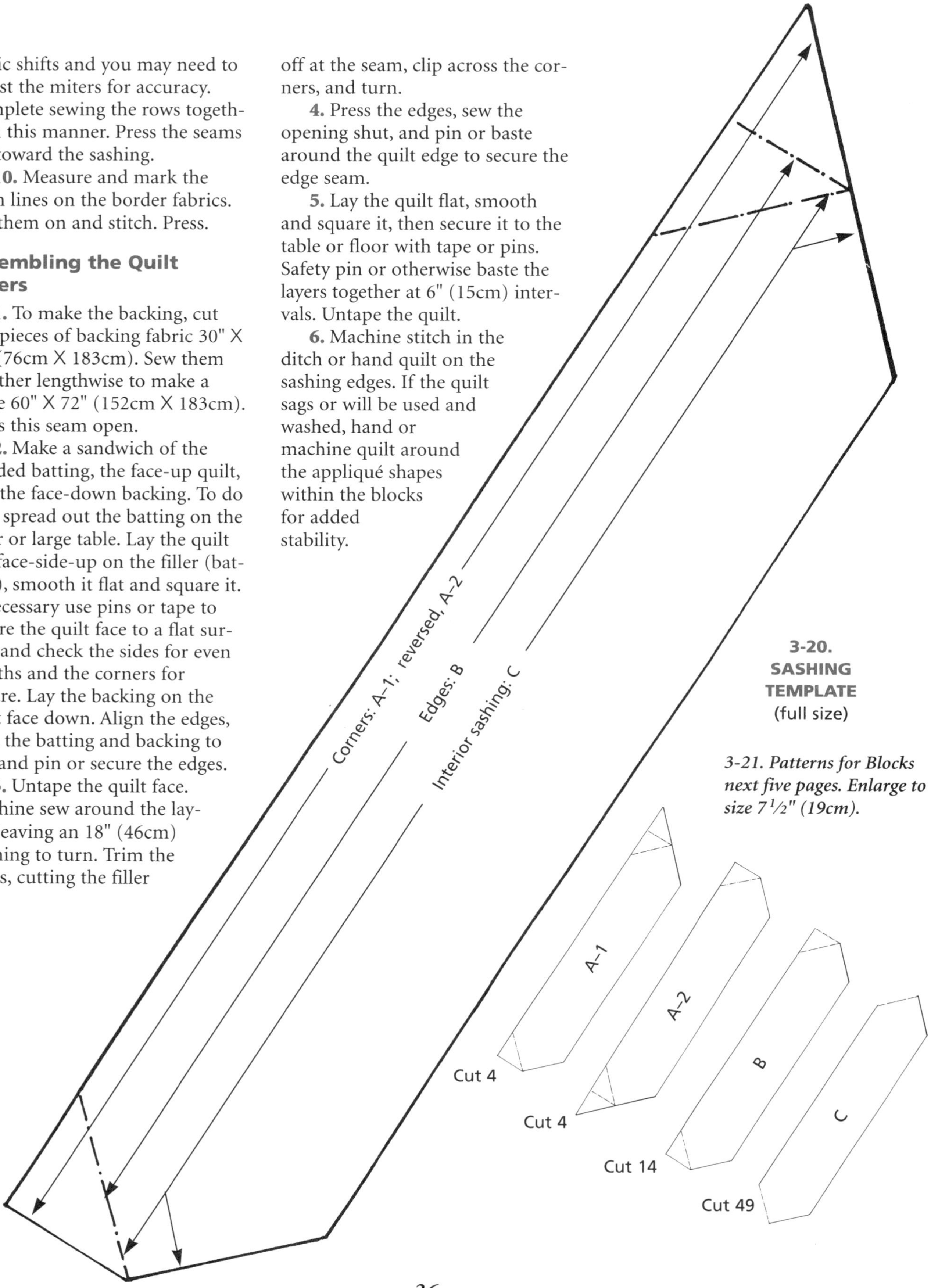

Corners: A-1; reversed, A-2
Edges: B
Interior sashing: C

3-20. SASHING TEMPLATE (full size)

3-21. Patterns for Blocks next five pages. Enlarge to size 7 1/2" (19cm).

A-1
Cut 4

A-2
Cut 4

B
Cut 14

C
Cut 49

ABC OBJECTS QUILT. Letters of the alphabet are so familiar we can "read" them in many exciting shapes and forms. This quilt by the author features an alphabet with letters shaped like objects, such as the butterfly-shaped "B." See page 123 for directions on making this machine-appliquéd quilt. Size: 38" X 42" (96.5cm X 106.5cm).

ABC ANIMAL QUILT. This children's quilt combines classic roman letters with animals—from "A" armadillo to "Z" zebra. The directions for making it, which start on page 31, feature a stacking-appliqué technique that makes it easier to appliqué the rather delicate letters. Size: 58½" X 71" (149cm X 179cm).

WELCOME BANNER. Old English lettering is combined with traditional heraldic colors and devices to make this modern, double-sided banner. The banner is made in weather resistant sport nylon. See page 48 for directions. Size: 20" X 64½" (51cm X 155cm).

GROW CHART. This spectrum-colored wall quilt makes it easy and fun to keep track of how fast your kids or grandkids grow. It features super-sized numerals in a wide-stroke type called Carousel and is made by piecing strips of fabric onto a backing with hidden seams. Directions for making it start on page 137. Size: 12" X 65½" (158cm X 33cm).

MONOGRAMMED TOWELS AND NAPKINS. Alphabet stitchery is an ideal way to create unique gifts your friends and family will treasure. You can personalize gifts with monograms, such as the circle monograms appliquéd on these towels. The napkins feature computer-generated, machine-sewn script lettering. See Chapter 6 for directions on designing and sewing monograms.

EVERY SILVER LINING HAS A CLOUD. You can use your favorite saying to design a sampler. Just design the letters on graph paper into a chart for sewing counted cross-stitch. Directions for this sampler begin on page 8. Size: 6½" X 9" (16.5cm X 23).

ZODIAC VEST. Using a computer sewing machine with memory cards, you can create a vest full of embroidered designs. Lacking that, do machine free-motion or hand embroidery. See page 66 for directions and a pattern for this vest.

MOTHER GOOSE QUILT. This quilt features a machine-embroidered nursery rhyme, a trapunto-stuffed appliquéd goose, and a background pieced in the traditional Flying Goose pattern. See page 130 for directions. Size: 41" X 45" (104cm X 114cm).

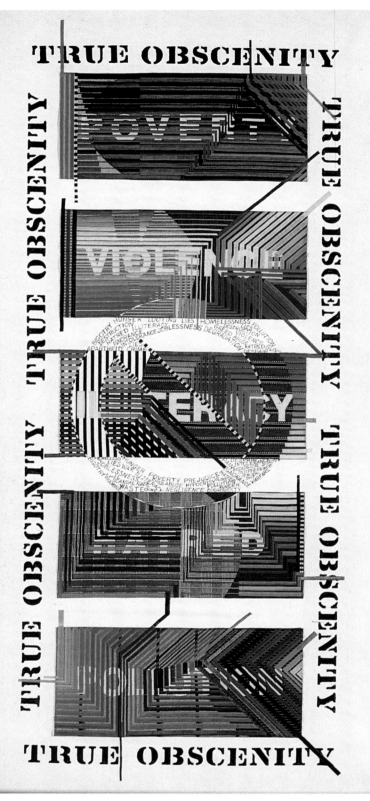

TRUE OBSCENITY. By B.J. Adams. Guest Artist B.J. Adams used a variety of lettering styles and techniques to communicate the message in the banner. Lettering styles include stencil, block, and hand lettering, and the banner features appliqué, satin-stitch embroidery, and fabric printing. Size: 65" X 30" (165cm X 76cm).

MEETING THE WITCH. By Marianne McCann. Guest artist Marianne McCann appliquéd fat block letters, casually drawn, on this charming quilt. These are easy to use and suit the storybook character of this hand-sewn quilt. Size: 66" X 77" (168cm X 196cm).

RIVA III, MOTHER AND DAUGHTER. By Ruth Reynolds. Reynolds uses whatever works in her hilarious quilt scenes. This piece features graffiti-style appliqué and hand lettering, along with an assortment of print and plain fabrics, including iridescents and metallics. Size: 41" X 68" (104cm X 173cm).

CENSORED SUBTEXT. By B. J. Adams. Rainbow colors of satin-stitch overlay nearly hide the block-style lettering in this wall hanging, proving that sewing can produce artwork.

I AM WHAT I THINK. This quilt piece was created by the author for a group self-portrait exhibition. It uses cut-out fabrics, lace for hair, and machine-embroidered lettering. The author used all six Brother Pacesetter 7000 memory card type styles to sew the sensory words. Size 24" X 30" (61cm X 76.5).

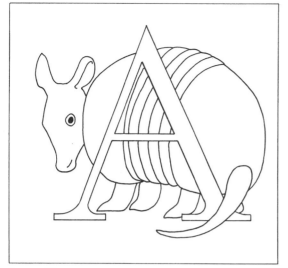

Armadillo

Butterfly

Cat

Dog

Elephant

Frog

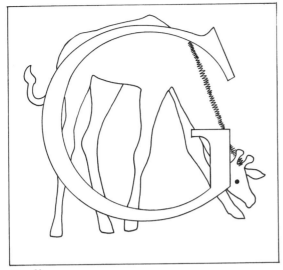

Giraffe

Hog

Iguana

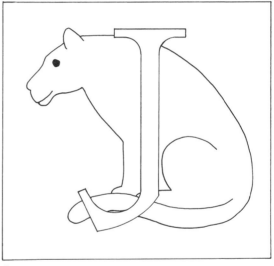

Jaguar

Koala

Lion

Monkey

Nuthatch

Ostrich

Penguin

Quail

Rabbit

Starfish

Turtle

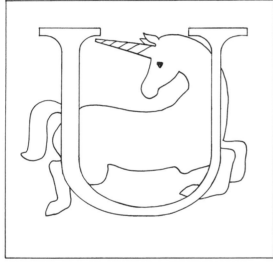

Unicorn

Vole

Walrus

Xiphosura (Horseshoe Crab)

Yak

Zebra

Sea

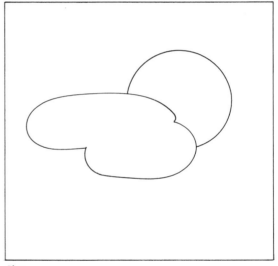

Sky

Plants

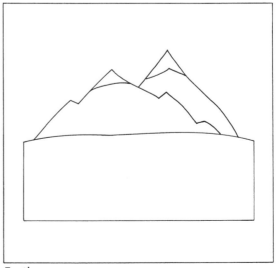

Earth

4-1. This "Welcome" banner features an Old English type style and several heraldic design elements. Constructed of sport nylon fabric, the double-sided banner is designed to endure weathering. Photo by Donna H. Chiarelli

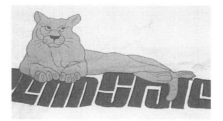

CHAPTER FOUR

Banners and Badges

Stitchers have been creating message-laden banners for hundreds of years. The messages appear sometimes in words, sometimes in symbols, and sometimes both. As a way of conveying messages, banners have many advantages. They are portable, visible from a distance, and when they feature symbols, they can surmount language differences. International road signs are one example of symbols that are used to convey a message: a diagonal line through a circle means no entrance, or forbidden. On banners, a pineapple means welcome, and a crown signifies royalty. Both symbols and words can speak to us. In fact, our letters and words developed from pictographs, which are drawn symbols of things, such as animals or people, and ideas.

Banners for identity appeared as early as the Old Testament, when every man of Israel was told to pitch his tent by his own standard, with the ensign of his

father's house. In the eighth century, Venerable Bede wrote that King Edwin of East Anglia rode about in war or peace with his standard-bearer carrying his emblazoned banner before him.

Heraldry developed as decorated shields and banners became an official means of identifying knights and leaders. This spread throughout western Europe during the twelfth century.

Nowadays we still love banners—at football games, tailgate parties, and in parades. We like to

4-2. Heraldic design elements are evident in the McGowan flag, shown here. It bears a whippet (the owner's high school dog) on the shield, a helmet crested with a cat, and an encircling motto scroll, all heraldic devices. UMAC is the owner's company emblem. Made and photographed by Lois Goodrich.

4-3. This Penn State flag, bearing the Nittany Lion logo, flies over the Peter Goodrichs' tailgate parties at Penn State games. Made and photographed by Lois Goodrich.

colored pencils or sheets of colored paper to experiment with different color combinations and shapes. Make small sketches and try several. When you've decided which to make, draw it on graph paper or enlarge it to size. Below, you'll find guide lines for lettering, type styles, color concepts, and fabric choices.

Heraldic Ideas for Banners

The banner project for this chapter incorporates some heraldic devices: divisions of bright color for visibility, the letter "H" for the family name, and a flower emblem for the garden. The crown and shield are simple geometric shapes harking back to heraldic imagery. The "Welcome" motto across the top also has a heraldic feel to it. Although it holds no claim to an official coat of arms, like traditional banners, this one conveys a message, as well: it hangs outside when the pool is open to invite the neighbors in.

Armory is the art and quasi-

hang them at home, too, to herald the seasons (showing snowflakes or flowers), celebrate holidays (Santa or a jack-o'-lantern), or make announcements ("It's a Girl!" or "Guess Who's Forty?").

Designing Your Own Banner

Heraldic banners, as well as banners, flags, and pennants from many other cultures and times, provide a wealth of design ideas for us to use today. See Fig. 4-4 for just a few of the shapes you can consider. The sky's the limit when it comes to symbols, messages, and sayings for your banner. You can use your dog, your house, a smiley face, or your favorite saying, for example. If you are designing your own banner, use

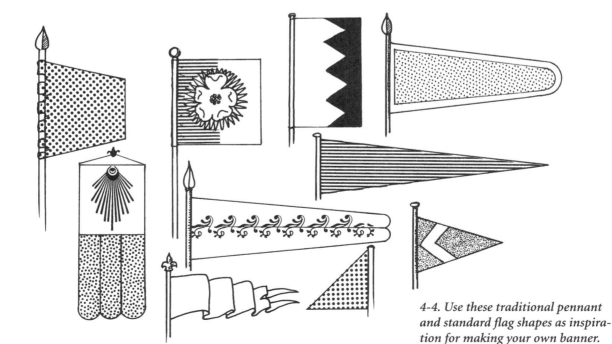

4-4. Use these traditional pennant and standard flag shapes as inspiration for making your own banner.

science of determining and designing armorial, or heraldic, bearings. If you would like to incorporate traditional heraldic emblems in a design, see Fig. 4-5 for some ideas to consider. Fig. 4-6 shows where these emblems fit into a coat of arms. For authentic and more extensive information on designing these, read *Basic Heraldry* by Stephen Friar and John Ferguson (The Herbert Press, U.K.), both members of the Society of Heraldic Arts.

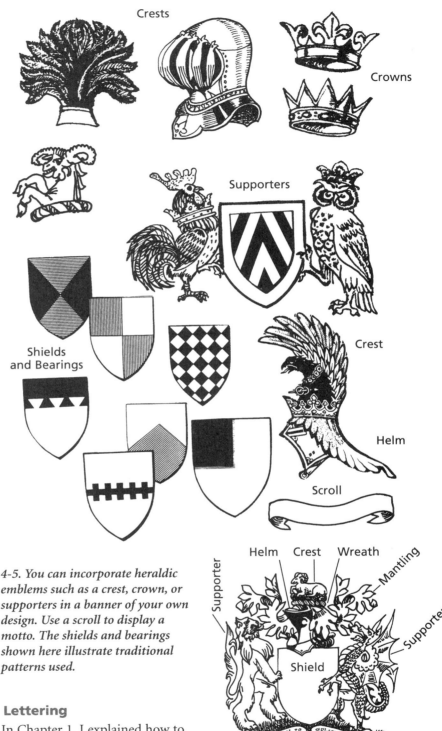

4-5. You can incorporate heraldic emblems such as a crest, crown, or supporters in a banner of your own design. Use a scroll to display a motto. The shields and bearings shown here illustrate traditional patterns used.

WHO GETS A COAT OF ARMS?

In England in 1483 it was determined that those elite who fought at Agin-court could have a coat of arms. (This eliminated a lot of us.) The granted coat of arms served as a symbol of service to the king and a way to identify family heritage. When armored families intermarried, emblems on the coat of arms were combined, with half the shield for him, the other for her. When their children married the shield was quartered, and so on.

Even though the British heralds still bestow coats of arms to those of provable genealogy or outstanding achievement, unofficially, anyone can create a personal banner using the general ideas of decorative imagery. Officially, no one may copy or use another's official coat of arms. (In 1577 William Dawkins was sentenced to whipping and loss of his ears for impersonating a herald and compiling false pedigrees.) Researching your ancestry may turn up a coat of arms—or a man with no ears.

Lettering

In Chapter 1, I explained how to draw letters on straight lines (see "Drawing Letters" and Fig. 1-9). But lettering on banner borders, cross bars, scrolls, or on pennants may need to fit into spaces other than straight, parallel lines. To fit letters to these shapes, draw guide

4-6. Traditionally, each coat of arms incorporates the crest, helm, wreath, mantling, supporters, shield, compartment, motto, and scroll.

4-7. Letters aligned around a circle or on a wavy line should remain at a consistent angle to the base line. Letters around a tight circle may need to be distorted in order to look right.

lines that follow the shape of the background. To read smoothly, the letters on these lines may need to be altered. On Fig. 4-7, for example, the top, bottom, and center guide lines remain the same relative distance apart, and the vertical letters always at right angles to the them. Script or italic letters maintain their consistent slant while following the curving guide lines.

On a pennant shape, the lettering often needs to diminish in size toward the tip—with letter tops, bottoms, and serifs slanted toward the tip, but all upright strokes a true vertical (see Fig. 4-8). To appear correct in a circle,

the letters must be wider at the tops than the bottoms, but all upright strokes must be aligned at right angles to the guide lines

from a central axis. On a wavy scroll, lettering has to conform to the edges, so letter heights all remain consistent, with strokes

4-8. Guide lines and lettering diminish as a pennant narrows. To create this effect, clip the lettering apart (top), then straighten the strokes with a guide (bottom).

University of Michigan

University of Michigan

4-9. Italic lettering angles to the right. It must remain at this consistent angle to the base line, even on curved or wavy lines.

ABCDEFG
HIJKLM
NOPQRS
TUVWXY
Z & abcdefg
hijklmnopq
rstuvwxyz

4-10. Old English Alphabet. Broad vertical strokes and delicate endings reflect the quill pens used to create this type style. Pressure on the pen widens the down stroke and narrows at the trail-off. These elaborate letters are commonly used as monograms.

vertical or at right angles to the base line, depending on which looks best (see Fig. 4-9).

With ready-made letters that cannot be remodeled, conform to the rules above as much as possible, and avoid extreme shapes such as tight circles, sharply angled pennants, or very wavy scrolls. Undistorted lettering will look awkward on these shapes.

Old English, one of the five basic type styles, is used on the banner below (see Fig. 4-10). This type style is elegant but difficult to read and create. Today it is used mainly for monogramming, invitations, and documents.

Colors

Bright colors are traditional on banners because of their visibility. Heraldry worked out certain rules for colors to achieve clarity, and they still work today, although we use many more colors. In heraldic terms, colors are classed as metals, tinctures, and stains. The metals are gold or yellow (called "or") and silver or white ("argent"). The tinctures are red ("gules"), blue ("azure"), green ("vert"), purple ("purpure"), black ("sable"), and mulberry ("murrey"). Stains include tawney ("tenné") and blood red ("sanguine"), and are rarely used. Traditionally, metal was never put on metal, nor tincture on tincture, for best visibility. This does not apply to adjacent colors and borders. Don't be surprised to find yourself making these same color decisions automatically when designing your own banner.

Fabrics

Due to the renewed popularity of banners and the current way of making them, special synthetic fabrics called tactical or sport nylon are now available in 60" (152cm) widths. This stiffly

MATERIALS AND SUPPLIES

The flag is pieced with no overall background color. To design your own, buy about 18" (46cm) of the 60" (152cm) width sport or tactical nylon in each color as I did for this banner. Amounts for it are listed below:

White fabric. 12" X 30" (30.5cm X 76cm) cut in three pieces.

Yellow fabric. 10" X 34" (25.5cm X 86.5cm) cut in two pieces.

Red fabric. 18" X 22" (46cm X 56cm) cut in two strips, four triangular tails.

Blue fabric. 12½" X 13" (32cm X 33cm) cut in two pieces.

Orange fabric. 18" X 26" (46cm X 66cm) cut in two pieces.

Green fabric. 10" X 16" (25.5cm X 40.5cm) one piece.

Purple fabric. 18" X 60" (46cm X 152cm); see below for cutting directions.

Threads. Polyester threads matching and contrasting to the colors above.

Tools and supplies. Ruler, 3" circle guide, pencil, zigzag sewing machine.

woven fabric allows for zigzag stitching the motif and color joinings with a minimum of pucker without using backing stabilizer. This results in a double-sided banner by trimming away fabric outside the stitch line on one side; inside the stitch line on the other.

Make the Pattern and Cut Out the Pieces

To make a pattern for the banner, use the measurements provided in Fig. 4-12. Then scale-up the pattern on a photocopier or graph. Scale up the pattern for the "welcome" lettering (see Fig. 4-11) so it is 13½" (35cm) long. In the steps below, you will draw or trace the shape on the right color fabric (use Color Fig. C-3 as a guide), and add seam allowances when you cut. Trace the motif patterns on the fabric but do not trim around them closely.

"WELCOME" BANNER

Overview. Like most banners, this one is made in bright colors with simple shapes for good visibility from a distance (see the Color Fig. C-3). Use the pattern given, or use the symbols provided in this chapter to design your own, adding whatever message you wish. Instructions for a two-sided banner are given, including how to avoid reverse writing on the back. Four different kinds of seams are detailed.

Technique. Double-sided appliqué, French seams, flat-fell seams, hidden seams. Or you can make all seams double-sided appliqué.

Type style. Old English. See Fig. 4-10 for the entire alphabet.

Size. 20" X 64½" (51cm X 162.5cm).

Color concept. Bright for visibility. Use the colors given or whatever is available at your fabric store.

Test Sew Your Fabric

Use scrap banner fabric and set your sewing machine for medium to wide zigzag (3.5mm), but not as close as satin-stitching (.8mm). Match the top and bobbin threads. Stitch on a double layer of banner fabric to see if the fabric pulls in at this setting. If so, narrow the stitch width. You can double stitch the outline for a fuller satin-stitch, but this, too, may pucker. Test on scrap until you achieve a good stitch line that is wide enough to hold the fabric when trimmed and dense enough to provide an outline of color, yet does not distort the fabric.

4-11

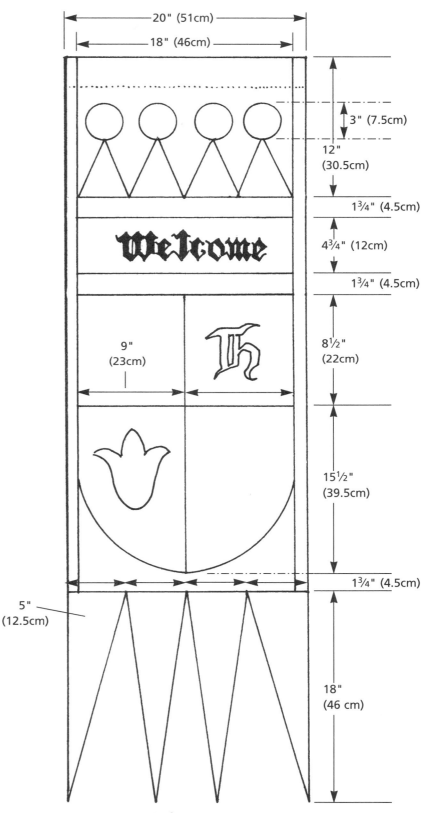

4-12. Welcome Banner Pattern

Appliquéing the Symbols

1. To appliqué the symbols, start at the top. Cut orange fabric 15" X 19" (38cm X 48.5cm), which includes a 3" (7.5cm) rod pocket at the top (2½" [6.5cm] finished width). Lay this fabric over the pattern. You will be able to see the pattern lines through it. Using a ruler and circle guide for accuracy, trace the pattern on the fabric. Align a strip of yellow 9-½" X 18" (24.5cm X 46cm) on the back of the orange so the pattern lines fit within the yellow. Pin in place outside the stitch lines.

2. Use red thread in both the top and the bobbin, with the machine set as to your test. Sew through both layers, centering the zigzag over the drawn lines of the pattern.

3. Use appliqué or sharp embroidery scissors to trim close to the stitch line (see Fig. 4-13). On the top, trim away the orange fabric inside the stitch lines to expose the yellow behind. Separate the fabrics to avoid cutting the underneath one. On the back side, trim away the yellow outside the stitch line. If you clipped a few threads, overstitch the zigzag lines to fill in the satin-stitch and reinforce any clipped threads.

4. Repeat for the flower section, with orange on top of the yellow background, using red threads.

5. For the initial letter, ("H" in my case) enlarge and trace your own letter from the alphabet in Fig. 4-10. Lay the paper tracing

4-13

over purple fabric, cut just larger than the letter. Then align both on the white fabric and pin in place.

6. Using purple thread on top, and white in the bobbin, sew a narrow zigzag following the paper pattern lines. Tear off the stitch-perforated paper pattern. Set for zigzag appliqué, as above, and sew the letter (see Fig. 4-14).

7. Trim outside the stitching, on the front only, and re-sew (see Figs. 4-15 and 4-16). Repeat for any other emblem you use with the darker color on top.

8. To make the "Welcome" lettering, repeat Steps 5 through 7. For lettering, do not trim away the white on the reverse side. Since this is a double-sided banner, make two equal white strips, with lettering centered on each. Align them back-to-back. Light shows through the banner, but the aligned words are so compact this is generally not significant.

Assemble the Banner

For various reasons, four different kinds of seams were used to assemble this banner: flat-fell, hidden, French, and double-sided appliqué. Directions follow, beginning at the banner top.

Flat-fell seam. A flat-fell seam

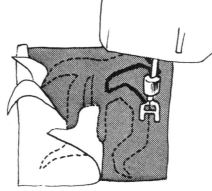

4-14. For accuracy, sew through a paper pattern for the initial letter, then tear away the stitch-perforated paper. Zigzag over the basting line.

joins the first two pieces (see Fig. 4-17). Draw light seam lines on the back of the banner pieces. Align drawn seam lines of the assembled yellow-orange top section with the red strip face-to-face. Straight stitch on the drawn seam line. Trim one seam allowance ³⁄₁₆" (4mm) wide. Fold a narrow hem in the other (which is about ½" [1.3cm] wide), and iron it toward the darker color over the seam allowance. Topstitch with matching threads. Repeat the flat-fell seam to join the second red strip lower on the banner.

Hidden seam. A hidden seam joins the red strip to the two white "Welcome" strips. Draw light seam lines on the back of the banner pieces. Align the red between

4-15. Use duckbill scissors to cut away the excess fabric around an appliqué letter without cutting the background fabric.

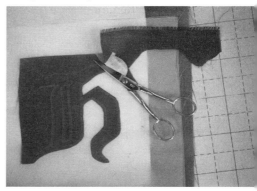

4-16. Detail of finished letter "H." You can double-stitch the zigzag stitching for a bolder outline.

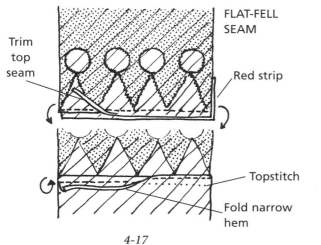

FLAT-FELL SEAM

Trim top seam

Red strip

Topstitch

Fold narrow hem

4-17

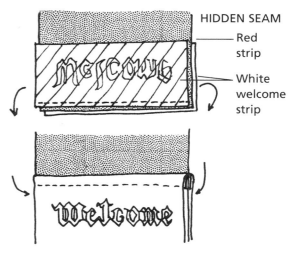

HIDDEN SEAM

Red strip

White welcome strip

4-18

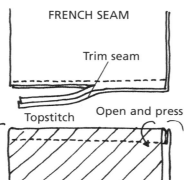

FRENCH SEAM

Trim seam

Topstitch

Open and press

4-19

the two white strips face-to-face on the front and face-to-back on the back. Then pin and sew. Trim all three seam allowances to ³/₁₆" (4mm). Fold the white strips down over the seam, sandwiching the seam allowances inside, and iron flat. Topstitch along the trimmed seam allowance line (see Fig. 4-18).

French seam. To French seam the top blue-and-white shield sections, draw seam lines on the front of the pieces. Align the sections along the vertical seam, back-to-back. Straight-stitch the seam. Trim the seam allowance to ³/₁₆" (4mm). Open the seam, press, and fold the pieces together. Press. Topstitch on the reverse side along the trimmed seam allowance (see Fig. 4-19). Repeat to join the yellow and green. Repeat again to join the blue/white to the yellow/green.

Double-sided appliqué seam. This type of seam joins the shield to the purple fabric. Cut out the shield pattern with ½" (1.3cm) seam allowances. Align and pin the purple in place on the green and yellow shield both face up. Zigzag the joining. Trim away the excess fabric very close to the seam line front and back, and zigzag again if needed (see Fig. 4-20).

Add Side Strips and Tails

1. For the side strips, cut the purple fabric into two full length strips 3¼" (8cm) wide. Fold purple strips in half lengthwise. Align each face-to-face with a side edge of the banner, checking the banner width measurement from the center line as you pin the border in place. Straight-stitch the border in place. Trim the banner and inside border seam allowances to ³/₁₆" (4mm). In the border seam allowance, fold a hem, press flat to form a flat-fell seam, and topstitch.

2. Measure and cut out the red tails with ½" (1.3cm) seam allowances. Hem the edges, except the top. To join the tails, align and pin the tops carefully face-to-face

on the purple banner bottom edge. Seam. Trim away the red seam allowances. Flat-fell seam the purple seam allowance and topstitch.

3. To make the rod pocket press a ½" (1.3cm) hem under. Turn a second hem 2½" (6.5cm) from this. Topstitch a double row of stitching ¼" (6mm) apart. You're done! Insert a dowel rod for hanging.

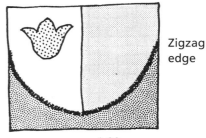

DOUBLE-SIDED APPLIQUÉ SEAM

Cut away excess fabric close to seam

Zigzag edge

4-20

5-1. **The Zodiac Emblem Vest,** *is embroidered on velvet, metallic fabrics, and exotic prints. It takes advantage of programmed, automatically sewn designs and was created using the New Home Memory Craft sewing machine.*

CHAPTER FIVE

The Amazing Sewing Machine

The sewing machine has come a long way in 150 years. The first mechanical sewing machine, invented in France in 1841, caused a riot among tailors, who promptly destroyed it. Undaunted, innovators such as Isaac Singer went on to perfect a workable sewing machine. Machines could sew stronger, more even, and much faster stitches than anyone could sew by hand, and tailors perceived them as a threat. Home sewers took to these mechanical marvels right away, though, and soon were making clothing, quilts, and other creations. Eventually, the tailors followed suit. Remnants of the battle exists today between hand-quilters and sewing machine users. Nevertheless, sewing machine manufacturers keep improving and inventing new sewing machines with amazing capabilities.

Today, there are sewing machines made for automatic pattern stitching, serging, chain stitching, embroidering, blind hemming, quilting, couching, heavy commercial work, computer-generated designs, and more. You can even create your own designs or generate them on your personal computer, attach a compatible sewing machine and it will sew them. Top-of-the-line machines also have come to the rescue of anyone who wants to sew letters. Almost every manufacturer offers machines with electronic brains that will sew well-formed letters for you.

This chapter explores the capabilities of these remarkable machines. You will find information on them interspersed throughout this chapter, along with a series of projects that highlight some of their best features. If you don't have one of these marvelous new machines, you can still adapt the projects to conventional machines or even hand sewing.

About Electronic Sewing Machines

For this book, several companies let me try their letter-generating computerized sewing machines. I spent hours studying the manuals, and more hours trying their special range of features. Then, I spent some very enjoyable time designing projects for them. In the end, I loved them all (well, almost) and showed them off to everyone.

I discovered that each company chooses to emphasize different aspects. For example, the Singer Quantum CXL sews script lettering sideways—continuously—as programmed (Fig. 5-2 shows it in action). The New Home Memory

Craft 8000 sews monograms sideways with an automated hoop, but it sews hand-guided lettering upright (see Fig. 5-3). Elna 9000 will make hand-guided letters and sews beautiful circles (see Fig. 5-5).

Several new models have attached hoops to move the fabric automatically and scanners to copy letters or designs in the machine's memory. Brother Pacesetter 7000, which has an attached hoop, has six different typefaces in three sizes on a disc that you put into the machine

(see Fig. 5-6). The new Viking #1, shown in Fig. 5-7, can sew 4" (10cm) letters with an automated hoop. Pfaff makes five kinds of letters, or allows you to design your own by manual programmer or on your PC with their program. Bernina Inspiration Plus 1630 has the computer mouse ball built into the machine.

How Computer Machines Work

Computer sewing machines don't actually compute. They have an

electronic board inside that directs their actions. On some simpler machines you don't know the electronics are there. On others you program a small screen to sew preset stitches like straight-stitching and zigzag, as well as many complex pattern stitches including overcasting, blind hemming, elaborate embroidery and lettering. Formerly mechanically driven, these patterns are now electronically programmed. Stitches can repeat continually, or perform one task at a time: making buttonholes, forming designs, or creating letters.

All these machines have a multitude of wonderful features that aren't given full credit here, since this book focuses mainly on lettering sewn on fabric. The projects in this chapter are designed to take advantage of these machine's lettering talents. To tell you all about their other workings would take an entire book, and does—each machine comes with an extensive manual showing what it can do. These booklets tend to emphasize delicate embroidery and monogramming. See Chapter 6 for monogramming and Chapter 7 for small lettering. Most projects in this book feature larger lettering so you can see what's going on—and because I like to make big stuff.

Only a certain amount of the machine's electronic capacity is devoted to built-in lettering. My Mac computer, for example, has 35 fonts (typefaces or variations of them) in many sizes, and no home sewing machine can match that. Some companies solved this problem by providing memory cards for lettering or emblems. The *Zodiac Emblem Vest* in this chapter, for example was made on the New Home Memory Craft 8000. The letters came from Memory Card 1, the zodiac

5-2. The mitten project in this chapter was designed with an all-in-one piece pattern to take advantage of the fact that the Singer Quantum CXL can embroider continuously—it just keeps on stitching.

designs from Memory Card 2. Other machines allow you to attach scanners to import letters or hook up to a PC computer—to sew all those thirty-five fonts in the foreseeable future. Keep in mind that computer sewing machines do not have a spell-check program (alas, if you spell like me) so double-check your spelling on lettering!

Deciding What to Buy

In the final analysis, there's no simple answer to which one to buy. I must confess the machine I liked best because of its smooth mechanics wasn't the best letterer. When friends asked me to recommend a machine to them, I felt like "Hello, Dolly" trying to arrange suitable marriages. "What do you want? Easy instructions? Best lettering? Super button-holes?" I'd ask. My solution was to sew as many lettering projects on each as time permitted to show what they can do. I have also included a list of questions you can use to evaluate all the machines—see "Questions to Ask Before You Buy." Now you can decide what's best for you.

Words to the Wise

Aligning and guiding fabric in these machines as they sew can be a challenge. You'll need to practice to get the effect you want. Before you begin sewing any project with these machines, plan your overall design and mark the perimeter guide lines with tailor's chalk, disappearing marker, or basting stitches on the fabric. Mark guide lines for the lettering to give you an idea of how much space it will take. (Most machines come with clear plastic printed guides that show sewn-pattern and lettering size.) If you are using a machine with an attached hoop, begin by fixing the panel in the automated

5-3. The New Home Memory Craft 8000 makes pre-programmed monograms, which you can alter by moving the hoop to change the effect.

QUESTIONS TO ASK BEFORE YOU BUY

What can this machine do? First decide what you want to sew—heavy denim, fragile lingerie, machine embroidery, or satin-stitch lettering, for example. Next, decide what you want the machine to do—be portable, sew quietly, letter automatically, or perform other automatic steps to ease your hands, perhaps. Then, look for a machine that does these best.

How much does the machine cost? Your choices can range from a $200.00 sale machine that does two or three stitches to a top-of-the-line machine that will do scores of stitches and tasks. The top-of-the-line machine can cost anywhere from $2,500.00 to $4,000.00. But don't think you have to get the most expensive machine to be happy: a $600.00 machine can do many tasks, and may be perfect for you.

What's a good compromise machine? Try to balance how much you can spend against what the machine can do and buy the best machine you can afford. Only the high-cost machines can embroider elegant automatic lettering. Low-cost machines may not be mechanically smooth or versatile.

Can I test-drive the machine? Take in your own fabric to see how the machine performs. See if it "feels right" to use. If possible, try different brands so you can compare them.

Is the manual easy to use? Some manuals are more "user-friendly" than others. The clearest for me was the Singer CXL which shows steps in 1-2-3 diagrams, making programming easy to do. More complicated machines have thicker user manuals, a necessary item for getting the most out of your machine. Follow a few steps in the manual to see how clear it is. Complicated machines need thick manuals, but they should be clearly written and well illustrated.

How can I get help? Ask about dealer services that are available. A good dealer will make sure you can handle the machine and provides reliable service. They may also give lessons or classes.

What about repairs? Ask about the machine's warranty before you buy. If the machine you buy needs service, only deal with authorized repair shops. If possible, take it to the dealer of your brand.

5-6. This emblem was created by sewing a roman-style letter "B" in the widest satin-stitch and encircling it with a wreath. It was sewn using the Brother 7000 automatic memory disks.

5-4. The new sewing machines can be used for a wide variety of projects. These Singer automatic-embroidered napkins were made on hemmed, 20" (51cm) square dinner napkins. The lettering was designed to fit on the top of the napkin when folded. Photo by Donna H. Chiarelli.

5-5. These examples were sewn on an Elna machine, which will sew block-style lettering with connecting stitches in between.

machine embroidery hoop. On machines with automatic lettering where your hands guide the fabric, you can use a separate machine embroidery hoop to keep fabric taut. Use a stabilizer, too, if necessary to keep your fabric from puckering.

Always test a sample of your fabric (and each combination of fabrics) before you sew the final project. Different fabrics will affect the stitching and thus the shape of the letters, so most machines have a stitch adjustment to offset this. You will need to stabilize some fabrics before you sew; otherwise satin stitching will pucker the fabric. The heavyweight canvas used for the *Embroidered Garden Tote* resisted the puckering pull of the machine embroidery, but some of the other fabrics required extra support to keep them from puckering. If your fabric puckers when you try some test embroidery, use stabilizer on the back or pin on tear-away backing. You can also fuse on a lining fabric when the embroidery is done to smooth it.

Lettering can vary from the pattern due to the type of fabric, how you guide the fabric, or if the fabric is being pushed out of line by hitting something—a cone of thread or the machine itself, for example. These machines have an adjustment to help shape the letter. You'll have to move the junk around your machine out of the way yourself.

Use good quality embroidery threads, Sulky or Janome New Home, for example. Others will break or tangle. For the bobbin, use a special bobbin thread that is thinner and gets more on the bobbin. With horizontal bobbin machines especially, be sure you have enough thread on the bobbin to complete the design you are working on.

It's also important to keep a good supply of the right needles for your machine on hand for embroidery. I went through a lot of them experimenting with these machines. Always change a bent or dull needle immediately. (You will find a guide to needle types in Chapter 2.) Use a new needle for best results. Be sure the needle is properly seated in the machine with the holding screw tightened.

That's all the warnings for now. Let's get busy and sew some projects!

5-8. These mittens were designed to be cut and decorated in one piece to take advantage of the way the Singer CXL sews a variety of built-in automatic patterns.

MITTENS

Overview. This project was especially created for sewing machines such as the Singer Quantum CXL, which stitch automatic letters and designs "sideways" (see Fig. 5-2). The lettering technique used here can be adapted to make placemats, Christmas stockings, or clothing. The pattern is designed so both mittens are cut in one piece, which allows the automatic stitching to be sewn in continuous rows across both mittens. The lining, added before stitching, acts as a stabilizer for the stitching. The double mittens are cut apart and assembled after decorating. The pattern given fits a 4-year-old child but can be scaled up to fit anyone.

Technique. Automatic machine embroidery.

Type style. Automated script, automated block (near tip).

Size. Child or adult, scale to size, as described below.

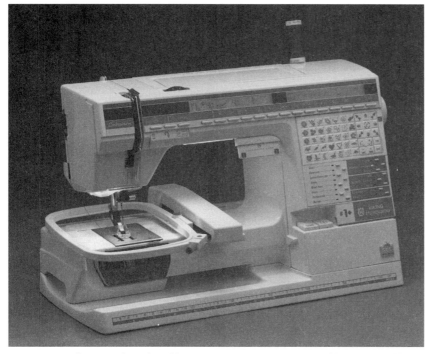

5-7. Sewing large embroidered letters requires an automated hoop as well as a program disc. Several machines now have this technology, including the Viking Husqvarna.

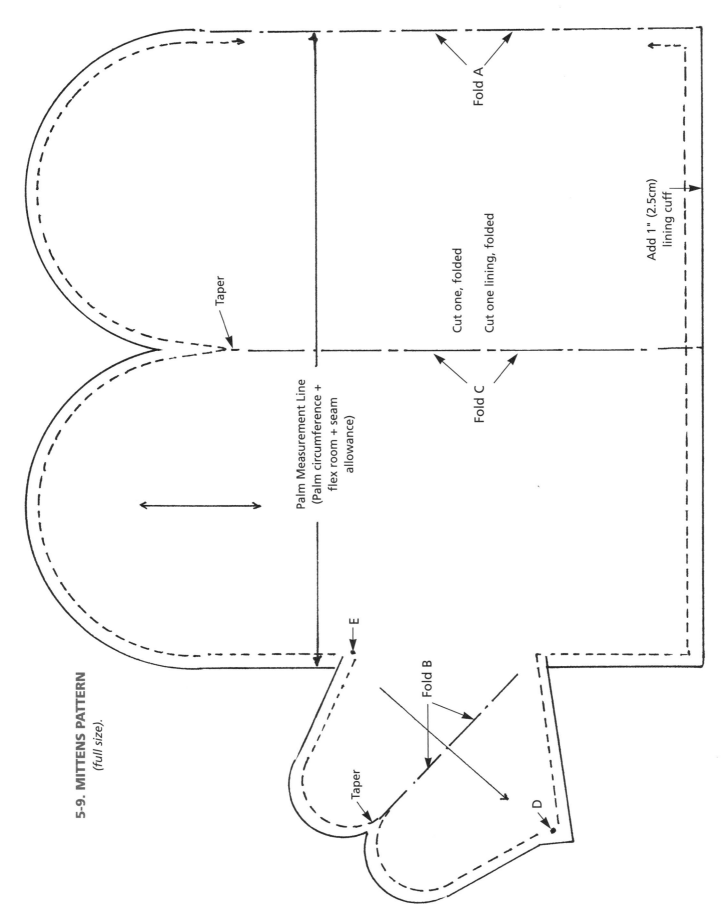

5-9. MITTENS PATTERN (full size).

Fold A

Taper

Palm Measurement Line
(Palm circumference +
flex room + seam
allowance)

Cut one, folded

Cut one lining, folded

Fold C

Add 1" (2.5cm)
lining cuff

E

Fold B

Taper

D

Making and Cutting Out the Pattern

1. The pattern given fits a child's palm, 6½" (16.5cm) around. To make it larger, measure around the palm of the hand to be fitted. Add about 1½" (4cm) for flex room and ¼" (6mm) seam allowances. Add less flex room for small hands, more for larger. For example, my hand circumference measures 7" (18cm) plus 1½" (4cm) to make a pattern 8½" (22cm) across the palm.

2. Mark a Palm Measurement Line (equal to palm circumference, plus flex room, plus ¼" seam allowance) on graph paper. Scale up the mitten pattern proportionately. (See "Scaling and Transferring" in Chapter 1 for directions on how to do this.) Transfer pattern markings to the paper pattern.

3. Lay the pattern with the grain of the fabric, pin and cut out both right and left mittens in one piece (joined at Fold A). Cut the lining the same way, except add 1" (2.5cm) or more at the bottom to make the cuff.

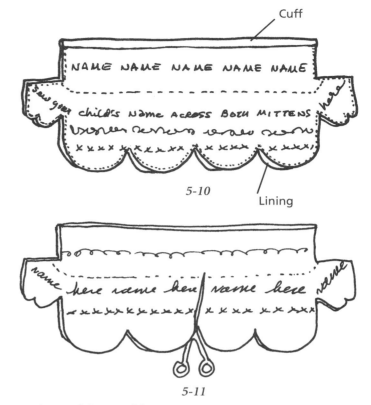

Cuff

5-10

Lining

5-11

Decorate and Assemble the Mittens

1. Before you decorate the mittens, add the lining, which serves as a stabilizer for the outer mitten fabric. To do this, align the outer mittens and the lining face-to-face along the cuff (flat) edges. Stitch across with a ¼" (6mm) seam allowance. Open the seam, and fold the lining back over the seam allowance to form a cuff (see Fig. 5-10). Align the mittens and lining back-to-back exactly and pin. Stay stitch around the raw edges, if needed.

2. To decorate, draw chalk guide lines across both mittens where you want to sew decorations. Angle the lines across the thumbs, as shown in Fig. 5-10. Machine stitch designs across the mitten. My mittens feature Hattie's name in automatic lettering, various automatic machine patterns, and some double-needle automatic patterns. Experiment with your machine's capacities.

3. Cut the two mittens apart as shown in Fig. 5-11.

4. To make the thumb, fold it wrong-side-out at Fold B. Match dots D and E (see Fig. 5-12) to

MATERIALS AND SUPPLIES

Fabric amounts. Outer mitten; child's size about 9" X 20" (23cm X 51cm) purple loose-weave fabric. Lining: 10" X 20" (25.5cm X 51cm) soft white fabric. Adult mittens take about 12" X 24" (30.5cm X 61cm); lining 13" X 24" (33cm X 61cm). To be more accurate, make your pattern to size then measure it for fabric amounts.

Recommended fabrics. Select a heavy-weight, woolly fabric for warmth for the outer mitten; a soft, somewhat thinner fabric for the lining. Or choose a tightly woven, wind- and water-repellent fabric over an interfacing and add a soft, warm fabric for the lining after embroidering. Stay-stitch around fraying fabrics.

Tools and supplies. Sewing machine that does automatic stitching; machine-embroidery threads in white, dark purple, pink; double sewing machine needle; scissors.

align the side seams. Using a short stitch length, sew the seam between the dots on the pattern. Taper the stitch line to make a rounded end. Clip to the stitch

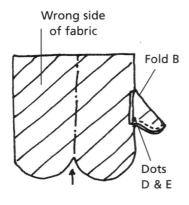

Wrong side of fabric

Fold B

Dots D & E

5-12

line at the base of the thumb—dot E.

5. Fold the mittens at Fold C to align them, lining side out, and include the thumb-edge in the seam (see Fig. 5-13). Using a short stitch, sew around the mitten from cuff top to tip, tapering at the end. Overcast this seam to reinforce it.

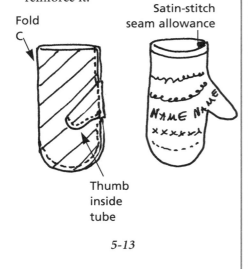

Fold C

Satin-stitch seam allowance

Thumb inside tube

5-13

6. Turn the mitten right-side-out. Cover the exposed seam allowances at the cuff with satin-stitching using matching thread.

7. To make the other mitten, repeat the process from Step 3.

QUICK-AND-EASY GIFT BAG

5-14. Dress up a gift with a stylish, easy-to-make gift bag that communicates your own message with machine-embroidered lettering. This wine bottle bag was sewn using the Viking Husqvarna 300.

Overview. Quick-and-easy fabric gift bags can be made in any size, color, or shape to suit the size of your gift. They are perfect for preserves, jelly, wine, candy, toys, or what have you. The message is machine embroidered in place, so it can be read when the bag is full. A bag made using the dimensions given here will wrap a bottle of wine.

Type Style and Technique. Automated script. Or simply apply lettering any way you wish.

MATERIALS AND SUPPLIES

Bag fabric. One piece of fabric 14" X 16" (35.5cm X 40.5cm) or as needed to fit the gift you wish to wrap.

Recommended fabric. Cotton, poly-cotton, corduroy, velveteen, denim, suede cloth—almost any scrap will do if it is firmly woven.

Ribbon. 24" (61cm) long X ¾" (2cm) wide.

Tools and supplies. Machine embroidery thread, scissors, pins.

Making Gift Bags

1. Cut one piece of poly-cotton or similar weight fabric that is in the size listed above. To make a pattern for a specific-size gift, measure around the object with a tape measure and add 3" to 6" (7.5cm to 15cm) so it will be easy to get objects in and out. To determine how tall your bag has to be, measure the height of the object and add that to its width, then add 5" (12.5cm) so there is plenty of room at the top for a hem and a tie ribbon.

2. Machine embroider your message vertically, below where the ribbon will be sewn on (see Fig 5-15). Or position it so it can be read when the bag is full. You can sew on one word or fill the entire bag with messages.

3. Hem the bag top. Fold the ribbon in half lengthwise, lay it on the face-up bag, and pin the fold across the seam line 4" (10cm) down from the top edge (see Fig. 5-15).

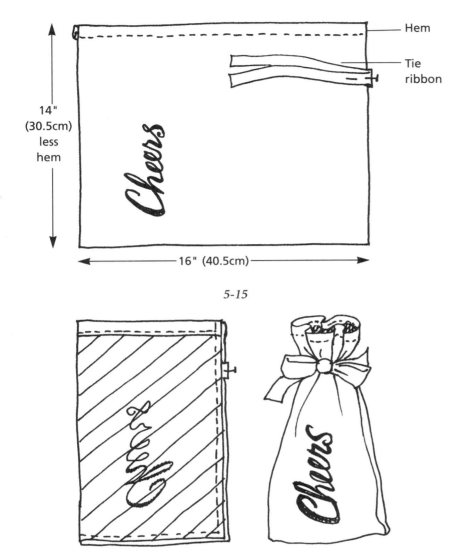

5-15

5-16

4. Fold the fabric face-to-face, covering the ribbon, and sew across the base and up the side. Sew the ribbon in place in this seam (see Fig. 5-16).

5. That's all there is to it. Just turn the bag right-side-out, insert your gift, and bring joy.

Using Memory Cards

Additional computer-programmed designs are available on memory cards, and these expand the electronic sewing machine's capacity. The final three projects in this chapter—the *Alphabet Sampler Purse, Zodiac Emblem Vest,* and *Embroidered Garden Tote*—all use memory cards, which are small plastic cards containing computer instructions for patterns and are inserted in a slot on the machine.

The larger letters and designs require a built-in, automated hoop for holding the fabric in perfect position while sewing, as well as a push button speed control.

Brother's roman-style letters create satin-stitched strokes as much as 7mm or 8mm wide—the whole letter is 1³⁄₁₆" (30mm) wide. Only two or three letters will fit within the frame at a time. (The latest Viking machine can make 4" [10cm] letters—the size of the entire hoop.) You need to release the frame and move the fabric to stitch additional letters.

Once programmed, the automated hoop moves the fabric in combination with the needle swing. It's eerie. You just push the button to begin, then sit back and drink a Coke while you watch it chug away. On a multicolor design, the machine sews a section, stops and tells you to change thread color, then continues. Who could get lonely with a machine that sends you messages?

It's fascinating to watch the letters form. The machine sews letters stitch by stitch in a certain order, as it has been programmed. It straight-stitches to the farthest point, satin-stitches back over this to the center, and repeats this technique until a beautiful letter is formed with no over-stitching.

The machine makes loose stitches to the next letter and sews it in the same manner. When the sewing is completed, the machine has a convenient thread clipper that cuts off both top and bobbin threads. When the embroidery is finished, you use curved embroidery scissors to clip away extra threads. If the item will be worn hard or washed, pull the thread ends to the back side, and use fray-checking liquid to prevent the threads from raveling; brands include Fray-Check, No-Fray, or STOP Fraying.

The difficult part of this type of machine embroidering is learning to position the hoop so the sewing appears where you want it. Machines with lettering capability

5-17. This closeup of the lettering on the Alphabet Sampler Purse *shows the automatic roman-style lettering of the Brother 7000, which is one of six letter styles available on memory disc.*

5-18. It required two memory disks to create the stitching on the Garden Tote Bag, *which was also sewn with at a Brother 7000.*

provide a stiff plastic sheet of letters and designs showing the completed sizes and the "needle drop," or where the letter starts to form. (The machine has a mind of its own, you need to remember.)

Begin with a guide line marked or even basted on the fabric. To locate the lettering on it, adjust the hoop placement using the stiff plastic centering guide that fits within the frame, the built-in "layout control," and a metric ruler to align lettering perfectly. The hoops do not have a large sewing area, so you need to move the fabric by changing the hoop to make longer wording.

Getting Started with Memory Cards

Before you start sewing projects, you will need to do some sample test lettering on your fabric. You'll need to keep a good supply of tear-away backing on hand. (Brother suggests using a paper coffee filter.) If you don't use it,

the wide satin-stitching of letters and large designs will pucker the fabric. Be sure to use enough backing to cover the entire wording you plan to embroider, so it won't fold or wrinkle on the back. You can also fuse on a lining fabric after the embroidery is done to smooth it.

Good-quality embroidery threads are important (Sulky or New Home, for example); otherwise your thread will break or tangle. For the bobbin, use a special bobbin thread that is thinner and gets more on the bobbin. With horizontal bobbin machines especially, be sure you have enough thread on the bobbin to complete the design you are working on.

Keep a good supply of assorted needles on hand and use a new needle for best results. Be sure the needle is properly seated in the machine with the holding screw tightened.

Once you've practiced a bit, you are ready to get started on a project. Let's start with one that doesn't require re-adjusting the hoop to complete the embroidery. In the *Alphabet Sampler Purse* and

the *Zodiac Emblem Vest* projects that follow, the letter sequences per row fit within the machine's frame, which makes positioning easier. Furthermore, the rows are pieced together, so you can make adjustments at this point, too.

Lettering the Purse

The letters are embroidered onto this bag before the pattern is cut out, so the fabric will fit in the hoop on the machine. If you choose to do this lettering free-motion or by hand sewing, scale up and trace the roman alphabet in Chapter 3, or use another alphabet of your choice.

To sew the lettering by machine, follow the directions below.

1. Align the blue velveteen in the hoop, select the letters on the machine in middle size and sew the letters "B" to "F" in gold machine-embroidery thread.

2. Realign, and sew "G" to "K" in fuchsia thread. Sew "L" to "O" in green, skip "P," and sew "Q" to "U" in orange, and "V" to "Z" in lavender.

ALPHABET SAMPLER PURSE

Overview. This purse features alphabet letters sewn in glossy, colorful machine-embroidery threads on rich velveteen. The letters are pieced by rows into a front panel. The lettering sequences fit within the automated machine's frame, so you can practice aligning the fabric. Believe me, it takes practice.

Technique. Machine programmed lettering, or any other kind you prefer. Patchwork assembly, allowing you to make a multicolored purse from scraps of fabric.

Type style. Roman programmed letters sewn on a Brother 7000.

Size. 8" X 8½" X 1½" (20.5cm X 22cm X 4cm).

Color concept. The purse is made of rich, medium-blue velveteen, which serves as the background color for the lettering in bright, lustrous embroidery threads. Black fabric and red welting are used for accents.

5-19. The Alphabet Sampler Purse is an ideal project for experimenting with automatic lettering. You could also make it from hand-guided machine lettering, if you like.

3. Sew the "P" on black velveteen. Why? The "L" to "P" line exceeded what will fit in the hoop (9cm), so to take advantage of a problem this letter was done differently as an accent.

4. Sew a large-size "A" in gold metallic thread on a 6½" X 4" (16.5cm X 10cm) piece of black velveteen for the fob.

5. Sew your name on the black back panel if you wish.

Make the Pattern and Cut Out the Purse

To make the pattern for this project, either measure directly on the fabric, or make a paper pattern for later use by scaling up the pattern given. Specific letter placement will depend on your sewing machine. NOTE: Measure and cut the lining and filler along with the bag pieces. A seam allowance of ½" (1.3cm) is included in these dimensions.

The pieces you need to cut out to make the purse are listed below.

Purse sides and bottom. Cut these pieces in blue velveteen, filler, and lining: 2 bag sides 6" X 9½" (15cm X 25.5cm); 1 bag bottom 2½" X 8" (6.5cm X 20.5cm) with rounded corners.

Purse back and top. Cut these pieces in black velveteen, filler,

MATERIALS AND SUPPLIES

Purse fabric. Purse front, sides and base: blue velveteen 10" X 20" (25.5cm X 51cm) minimum, or ¼ yd X 44" (23cm X 111.5cm) for experimenting. Purse back, top and fob: 9" X 9" (23cm X 23cm) black velveteen or suede cloth.

Lining. 10" X 20" (25.5cm X 51cm); choose fabric in a harmonizing—or surprising—color.

Recommended fabrics. Velveteen, denim, suede cloth, thin leather. Be sure to select a study fabric that wears well.

Filler. Bonded fiberfill, 10" X 20" (25.5cm X 51cm).

Welting and pull cord. 2" X 9" (5cm X 23cm) red velvet or other fabric for welting; 24" (15cm) decorative fuchsia cording for pull cord.

Threads. Machine embroidery threads in metallic gold, metallic green, gold, fuchsia, green, orange, lavender. Blue sewing thread.

Tools and supplies. Blue 7" (18cm) zipper, wire and jump ring, pliers, programmed sewing machine, scissors, tape, and ruler.

5-20. PURSE PATTERN

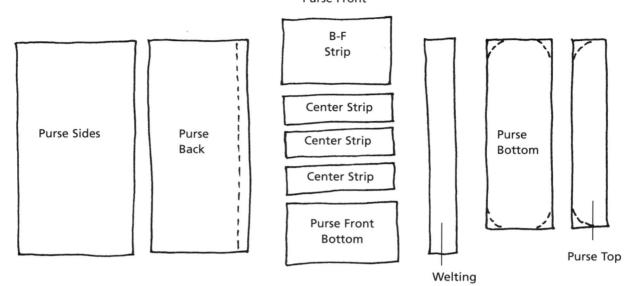

Purse Front

Purse Sides

Purse Back

B-F Strip

Center Strip

Center Strip

Center Strip

Purse Front Bottom

Welting

Purse Bottom

Purse Top

and lining: Bag back 5" X 9½" (12.5cm X 25.5cm); 2 bag tops 1¾" X 8" (4.5cm X 20.5cm)

Purse front strips. To cut out the pieces that have lettering on them, once the lettering is done, center it, and measure seam allowances on the top and bottom. Cut the B-F Strip 4" X 5½" (10cm X 12.5cm) with the lettering up ¾" (2cm) from the bottom edge. Cut the three Center Strips of lettering to 2" X 5½" (5cm X 12.5cm). Cut Purse Front Bottom strip to 3" X 5½" (7.5cm X 12.5cm) with the lettering down ¾" (2cm) from the top edge.

Fob. Cut the fob in black velveteen and filler using Fig. 5-21 as a pattern. Do not cut lining.

Assemble the Purse

1. Piece together the lettering panel as follows: sew the **P** to the **L-O** row, aligning the letters evenly. Align the **B-F** row with the **G-K** row, face-to-face, then stitch them together. Align and sew the **L-P** row. Join the **Q-U** and **V-Z** strips.

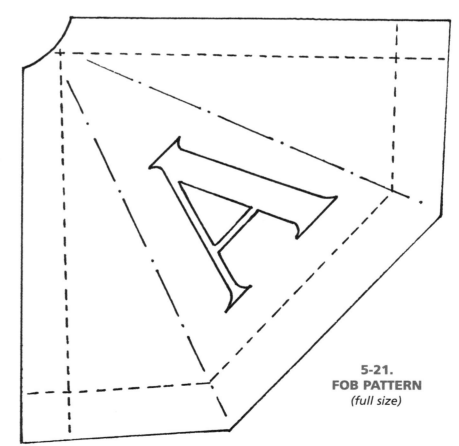

5-21. FOB PATTERN *(full size)*

2. Cut a piece of filler and a piece of lining, 5½" X 9½" (14cm X 24.5cm). Stitch the lettering to the filler in the ditch between the rows. (Set the lining aside until the bag is assembled.)

3. To make the welting, fold the red fabric strip over the 18" (46cm) cording and stitch with a zipper foot. Then pin the welting seam allowance to the alphabet panel on each side, aligning the welting stitch line with the seam line (see Fig. 5-22). Sew on the welting stitching line.

4. Align the sides, backed with filler, to the panel and welting and stitch. Align the back with filler to the sides and stitch (see Fig. 5-23). (The lining is set aside until the bag is assembled.)

5. With the bag still inside-out, sew a top strip on either side of the zipper. Fit the assembled top to the bag and sew (see Fig. 5-24). Open the zipper. Align the filler-backed base to the bag and sew.

Opening to turn bag

5-25

side-out, sew the opening closed, and tuck in the lining (see Fig. 5-25).

7. To make and attach the fob, measure a 6" (15cm) cord and double it. Lay the cord on the fob face with both ends out the top (see Fig. 5-26). Fold the fob as shown to align the edges. Sew the fob seam, catching the cord in the seam. Tuck in the cord and align the fob bottom edges. Sew ½" (91.3cm) from each corner. Turn by pulling on the cord loop. Stuff lightly with filler. Sew the bottom closed. Attach a large jump ring to the cord and the zipper pull to attach the fob.

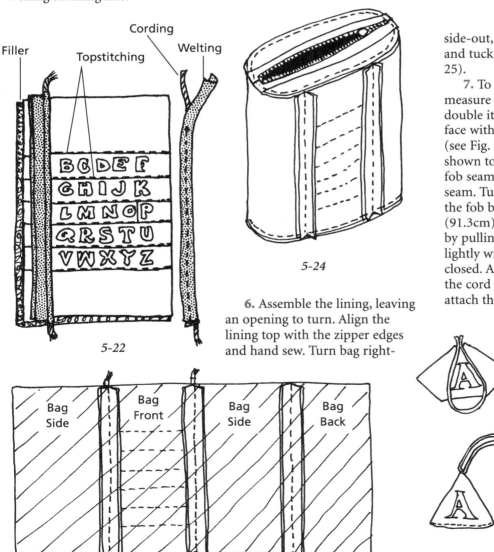

Filler Cording Welting Topstitching

BCDEF
GHIJK
LMNOP
QRSTU
VWXYZ

5-22

5-24

6. Assemble the lining, leaving an opening to turn. Align the lining top with the zipper edges and hand sew. Turn bag right-

Bag Side Bag Front Bag Side Bag Back

5-23

A

A

BCDEF
GHIJK

5-26

65

ZODIAC EMBLEM VEST

5-27. The Zodiac Emblem Vest was sewn on a New Home Memory Craft 8000 machine using two memory discs, one for the emblems and another for the lettering.

Overview. Vests are ideal projects for experimenting. They are decorative, small enough to use scraps of elegant fabrics, and they are relatively easy to construct. This basic pattern provides three essentially rectangular pieces for you to embellish any way you wish—with patching, decorative stitching, ribbons, or appliqué, for example. The pattern also allows for easy adjustment in size, both in length and circumference, and in shape as well.

Technique. This vest is made using crazy quilt style patchwork, which means that added pieces are appliquéd to a base fabric. The zodiac emblems were embroidered on a separate piece, patched into horizontal strips, then appliquéd to the vest. For a better fit on a full figure, add darts and plan the strips to incorporate them, making sure that the darts do not appear within the patches.

Type style. Automated Roman from New Home memory card 1.

Size. Materials given below are for an adult medium-size vest and make a 38" circumference vest, which includes ease for wearing over clothing. (The vest only skims the hip at the waist.) To adjust the size, measure the chest and scale the pattern up or down as needed, see "Adjust the Pattern" below for directions.

Color concept. Colors for this vest are deep and rich, as you can see from Color Fig. C-5. The patches are black with light, bright, and metallic threads for accent. The added fabrics are metallic weaves, prints in dark rich colors with metallic touches, and threads in warm bright colors. The vest back is a deep rust color and the sides are batik rust print. Your fabric choices will vary (one of mine was a friend's donated nightgown), so arrange them all together before assembly to achieve harmony.

Adjust the Pattern

To adjust the size of the pattern, measure the chest circumference of the person you are making the vest for. Add about 2" (5cm) of ease per piece as well as 1½" (4cm) per front piece for overlap for the buttons. Add ½" (1.3cm) seam allowances per piece. (For the 38" vest this totals 47" [119cm] around.) Use the "Sizing Chart" on page 68 to help you make the needed adjustments. NOTE: Dimensions of pieces on the chart include ease added to the chest measurement, but you add the seam allowances. Another way to adjust the size is to widen individual pieces as needed.

When you make your pattern, keep in mind that the vest back is unlined and includes a hem at the bottom.

You can make variations of other sorts, too, as shown in Fig. 5-28. To lengthen the vest, add inches to the horizontal adjustment marks. For a boxy vest, cut the vest front tips off evenly. For a fitted vest, shape the side piece and add a vertical dart as shown. For a variable side, insert ties or ribbons in the side seams and tie them to size as shown.

Cut Out the Vest

Once you've decided on the adjustments you'd like to make, scale up the pattern (see Fig. 5-29) to the size you need. Cut out the pattern and pin the pieces together to try it on for size and fit.

Select the fabric colors to create the effect you want. Then cut out the basic pattern pieces in selected fabrics as listed below. Do not cut out the background fabric for the emblem patches—you will embroider these before cutting them out.

Front. Cut 2 fronts in your regular fabric and 2 front linings.

Sides. Cut 2 sides in your reg-

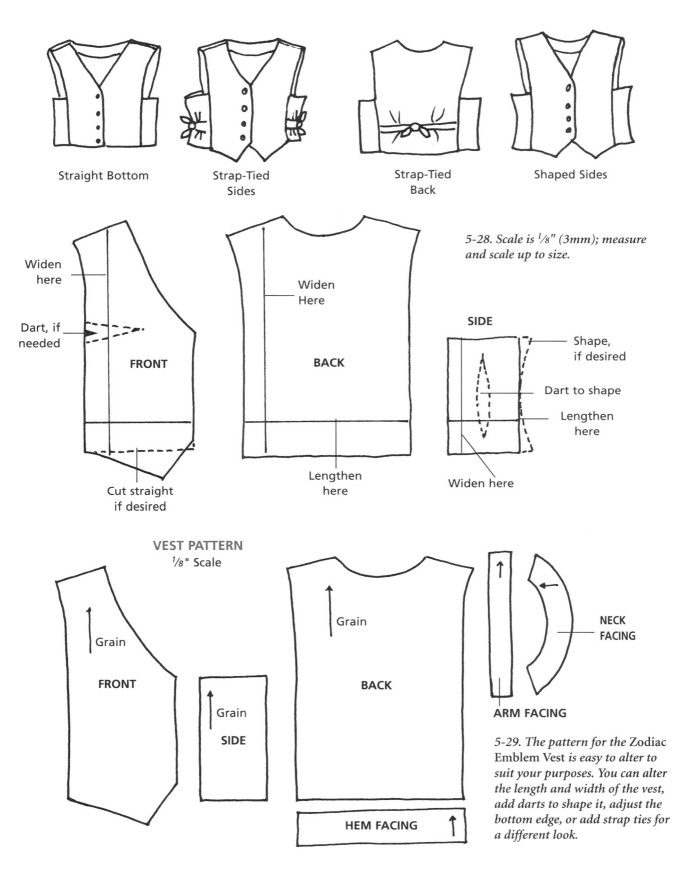

Straight Bottom

Strap-Tied
Sides

Strap-Tied
Back

Shaped Sides

Widen
here

Dart, if
needed

FRONT

Cut straight
if desired

Widen
Here

BACK

Lengthen
here

5-28. *Scale is* 1/8" *(3mm); measure
and scale up to size.*

SIDE

Shape,
if desired

Dart to shape

Lengthen
here

Widen here

VEST PATTERN
1/8" Scale

Grain

FRONT

Grain
SIDE

Grain

BACK

HEM FACING

**NECK
FACING**

ARM FACING

5-29. *The pattern for the Zodiac
Emblem Vest is easy to alter to
suit your purposes. You can alter
the length and width of the vest,
add darts to shape it, adjust the
bottom edge, or add strap ties for
a different look.*

SIZING CHART

The width of the pattern at the chest measurement line is listed below. Measurements include "ease," but do not include seam allowances: add ½" (1.3cm) seam allowances when you cut your pattern.

Size	Chest	Front	Back	Side	Total
CHILD					
Small	22" (56cm)	5.5" (14)	9" (23cm)	4" (10cm)	28" (71cm)
Medium	25" (63.5)	6" (15cm)	10" (25.5)	4.5" (11.5)	31" (79)
Large	28" (71)	7" (18)	11" (28)	5" (12.5)	35" (89)
ADULT					
Small	32" (81.5)	8" (46)	12" (30.5)	6" (15)	40" (101.5)
Medium	38" (96.5)	9" (23)	15" (38)	7" (18)	47" (119)
Large	42" (106.5)	10" (25.5)	17" (43)	7.5" (19.5)	52" (132)

MATERIALS AND SUPPLIES

Vest fabric. For the entire vest, including liners and back facings, you need 1 yd (91.5cm) firmly woven poly-cotton plain rust fabric.

Front lining. Two pieces 10" X 24" (25.5cm X 61cm) firmly woven poly-cotton.

Side panels. Two pieces firmly woven cotton batik print 7.5" X 12" (19.5cm X 30.5cm).

Emblem patches. About 18" X 24" (46cm X 61cm) black suede cloth or velveteen. Do not cut into squares; embroider first.

Strip patches. 18 pieces of metallic or print fabric 2" X 4" (5cm X 10cm).

Strips. Four strips print fabrics 2" X 9" (5cm X 23cm); additional strips as needed to cover fronts 12" X 9" (30.5cm X 23cm) in rust, gold, metallic, maroon and black print fabrics.

Threads. Use lustrous machine embroidery threads such as Sulky and Janome New Home. Use light, bright colors.

Fuser. 18" X 24" (46cm X 61cm) iron-on fuser to stabilize.

Pattern-making supplies. 24" X 24" (61cm X 61cm) white paper, pencil, yardstick, and measuring tape.

Tools and supplies. Computer sewing machine and embroidery hoop (or ways to apply letters such as skill at free-motion sewing or hand-sewing), sharp scissors, large-head pins, iron, fabric marking pencil.

ular fabric and 2 side linings.

Back. Cut 1 back in your regular fabric.

Facing. Cut 1 neck facing and 2 arm facings. NOTE: Before you cut out the neck facing, machine embroider a label or signature in it (see Fig. 5-30); you need enough fabric for the hoop to hold firmly.

5-30

Embroider and Piece the Vest Front

1. Determine where the designs will fit on the uncut emblem background fabric. You need space around the emblem to hold the fabric in an embroidery hoop for sewing. Each design takes about 4" (10cm) square with seam allowances, but plan for 6" (15cm), since machine hoop placement isn't always exact. Cut them apart later. Keep in mind that the size of the emblems sewn by machine cannot be varied. You will need to place them differently to fit them on smaller vests, perhaps on the back as well.

2. Stretch the fabric in a machine-embroidery hoop. Include a stabilizing backing to combat puckering. For free-motion embroidery, use a detached sewing-machine hoop. For hand sewing, use an embroidery hoop without stabilizer.

3. Embroider the designs. The programmed designs shown are from the New Home machine. You can scan in your own designs on many of the newest, computer-automated machines. Iron on a fused backing and tear off the paper backing.

4. Select harmonizing colors of

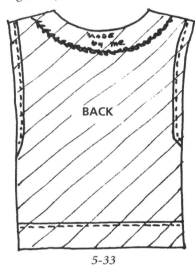

5-31

fabric strips, ribbons, and patches for the vest fronts. Then join the completed emblems and patches into horizontal strips, as shown in Fig. 5-31. A completed strip will contain five pieces: the adult medium size, for example, has a 1" (2.5cm) wide patch, a 3" (7.5cm) wide emblem patch, a 1" (2.5cm) patch, a second 3" (7.5cm) emblem patch and a 1" (2.5cm) patch to make a 9" (23cm) wide strip.

5. Lay out the vest liner fronts and arrange the strips to cover them. Pin the emblem strips in place and iron the fuser onto the lining. (Avoid too much heat on metallic fabrics; iron from the backside.)

6. Fold hems on the strips between them and topstitch in place (see Fig. 5-32). Lay other

added strips face down, seam in place, and fold back for hidden seams. Decorate the strips with automatic-patterned embroidery, couch-on cording, ribbons, beads, sequins, or whatever else you'd like to add to achieve the effect you want.

Assemble the Vest

1. Hem or serge the back neck and two arm facings. Align them to the vest back, right sides together, and sew on. Clip and grade the seam allowances, press, flip to inside, and topstitch in place (see Fig. 5-33).

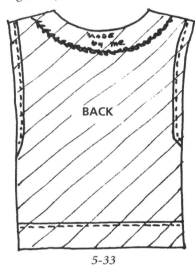

5-33

2. Fold up the hem on the vest back with a small turn-under at the top to hide the raw edge. Topstitch.

3. Align the side and its lining. Stitch the top and bottom seams. Grade the seam allowances, turn, and press (see Fig. 5-34). Repeat for the other side.

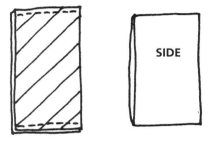

SIDE

5-34

4. Align the vest fronts face-to-face with the back. The unfinished front will extend beyond the finished back neck edge (see Fig. 5-35). Sew the shoulder seam.

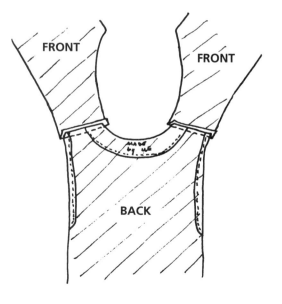

FRONT

FRONT

BACK

5-35

5. Align the front lining and the vest front face-to-face. Tuck the vest back inside these pieces, and sew all edges except the side

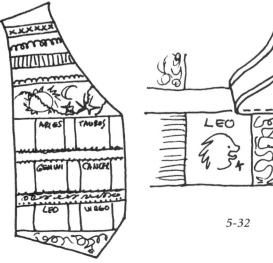

5-32

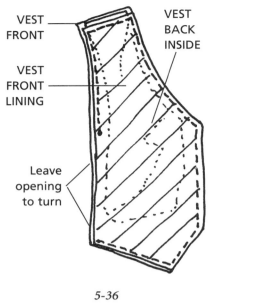

VEST
FRONT

VEST
FRONT
LINING

VEST
BACK
INSIDE

Leave
opening
to turn

5-36

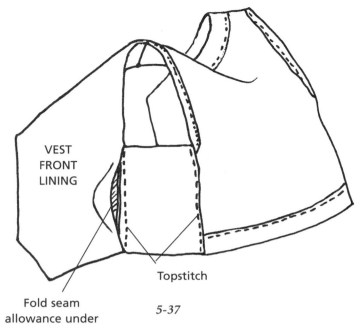

VEST
FRONT
LINING

Fold seam
allowance under

Topstitch

5-37

seam (see Fig. 5-36). Clip and grade the seam allowances, then turn by pulling the vest back out. Press.

6. Repeat for the other side, tucking in both the back and other front. Pull them out through the side opening to turn. Press and topstitch the edges.

7. To join the sides the easiest way, align the pieces face-to-face, and serge side seams. For more finished seams, align the front and the lined side face-to-face, excluding the front lining from the seam. Stitch, open flat, and press the seam allowance toward the vest front. Turn a hem in the front lining, pin in place to cover the lining seam, and topstitch or hand-sew closed (see Fig. 5-37). Repeat for the other front seam. Repeat for joining both back side seams.

8. Measure and sew buttonholes on the right side (when worn). Sew buttons on the left side.

EMBROIDERED GARDEN TOTE

5-38. The **Embroidered Garden Tote** *features machine embroidery on a tote bag pattern that you can adapt and decorate any way you wish.*

Overview. This project provides a sampler pattern you can use to practice hand or machine sewing techniques. It also includes a tote bag pattern for you to use and decorate as you like. If you don't want to use the sampler in a tote bag, consider using it on a purse, pillow, or clothing. You can also frame it or save it in a notebook for reference in later projects.

Technique. Automated machine embroidery.

Type style. Computer-programmed script. The example shown was sewn on a Brother 7000. You can also use other techniques and type styles to make the tote panel. (See Fig. 5-47 at the end of the chapter for a sample italic typeface page to use if you don't have a programmable machine.)

Size. Sampler panel is 11" X 14" (28cm X 35.5cm). Bag is 18" (46cm) wide, 17½" (44.5cm) tall (plus handles). The base is 6" X 14½" (15cm X 37cm).

Color concept. The stitchery is done on natural white canvass in flower colors—red, golden yellow, pink, purple, and blue—as well as leaf colors—light green, dark green, and pea green. The print fabric that covers the bag was selected to harmonize with the stitchery on the panel. It is a popular vegetable print in a riot of color, and fits the saying on the sampler.

Make the Pattern

The pattern for this bag is drawn directly on the fabric pieces. If you wish, make a paper pattern for use and keep it in your files. Use Fig. 5-39 as the pattern for the embroidered panel. Or plan your own lettering to fit in the center surrounded by flowers.

5-39

Although the finished size of the embroidered panel is 11" X 14" (28cm X 35.5cm, to make the panel, measure and cut a piece of canvas 14" X 18" (35.5cm X 46cm) to accommodate the embroidery hoop. Draw seam lines on the back, but do not trim it to size until after sewing on the designs (see Fig. 5-40). Cut the lining to

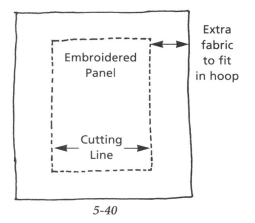

5-40

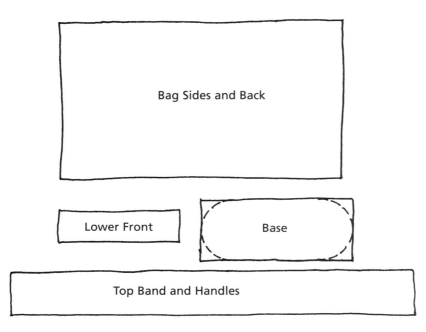

5-41

the finished size, 11" X 14" (28cm X 35.5cm).

Measure and cut the bag pieces as listed below, and as shown in Fig. 5-41. Seam allowances of ½" (1.3cm) are included in the measurements listed.

Bag sides and back. Cut one each of print fabric and canvas lining: 17" X 26" (43cm X 66cm).

Lower front. Cut one each of print fabric and canvas lining: 3" X 12 (7.5cm X 30.5cm).

Top band and handles. Cut two each of print fabric and canvas lining: 4" X 37" (10cm X 94cm). Use one set as the top band. Fold the other set in half to make two handles, 4" X 18½" (10cm X 47cm).

Base of bag. Cut one each of print fabric and canvas lining. To make a paper template pattern for the base of the bag, draw a 6" X 14½" (15cm X 37cm) rectangle on a piece of paper. Draw a center

line the length of it, then measure 3" (7.5cm) from each end. Using a compass, make a 6" (15cm) half-circle for each end. Trace the template on the lining, then add ½" (11.3cm) seam allowance all around the outside edge.

Align all lining pieces with their bag pieces and pin or baste together. Draw seam allowances on the linings.

Sew the Sampler Design

Start by doing some test embroidery on your fabric. If it puckers, use iron-on stabilizer backing or pin-on tear-away backing. If the layers are too thick for the hoop, place the paper backing beneath the hoop and add the lining after embroidering.

Mark design perimeter guide lines with tailor's chalk, disappearing marker, or basting stitches on the panel. Draw chalk or sew basting lines for the lettering. Trace the pattern if you plan to do free-

motion stitching or hand embroidery.

Sew the lettering first. Fix the panel in the machine embroidery hoop, use a separate hoop, or free-motion sew with your hands to guide the fabric and create the lettering. Then add the flowers. If spacing between letters is off, sew a flower between them: machine embroidery makes tight, tiny stitches, which makes mistakes hard to pick out.

Assemble the Bag

1. Align and sew the lined lower front to the lined embroidered panel. Serge the seam or overcast and trim to make a ¼" (6mm) seam. Press open and topstitch.

2. Align the embroidered panel and edges of the lined bag sides and stitch. Press to one side and topstitch the seam allowances to the bag (see Fig. 5-42).

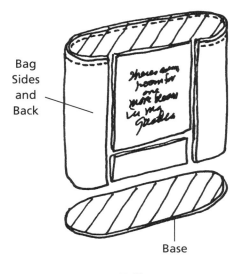

Bag Sides and Back

Base

5-42

3. Align the lined base to the assembled bag and panel. Pin through the drawn seam lines. Serge or overcast and trim the edges (see Fig. 5-42).

4. To sew the strap handles use a yardstick to draw a center line lengthwise on the handle lining. Align the strap and lining. Fold length-wise hems 1¼" (3cm) wide on each side to meet at the center line, and press. Then fold the

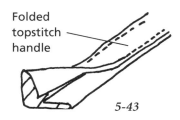

Folded topstitch handle

5-43

folded edges together and press (see Fig. 5-43). Topstitch in the same direction on each edge. Repeat to make the other handle.

5. To make the top of the bag, align the lined top band ends and seam them together to make a loop the same diameter as the bag (see Fig. 5-44). Fold double lengthwise—face side out, align this with the bag top edge, and serge or overcast.

6. To attach the handles, align the ends 5" (12.5cm) apart, centered on the design panel. Pin them to the band, and sew a 1"

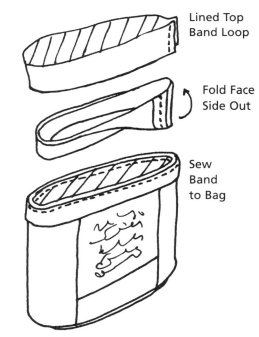

Lined Top Band Loop

Fold Face Side Out

Sew Band to Bag

5-44

5-45

Sew "X" to secure handles

(2.5cm) "X" to secure the handle (see Fig. 5-45). Fold the bag flat to match the handle location on the back side. Repeat to secure. Trim off the extra ends by serging or overcasting on the band/bag seam.

Scanning and Programming Patterns

The automatic lettering and designs built into electronic sewing machines or memory cards cannot, as a rule, be altered. Yet sometimes you want a different size letter or a different type style. The sewing machine companies keep inventing new ways to give you more options.

Some machines have a scanner accessory that will copy lettering or a drawing. This lets you convert your own drawing or borrowed art into stitching. Easy to say but complicated for the machine to do. In order to sew a

pattern in this fashion, it must program the order of sewing stitches and what stitch pattern to use. I used the New Home scanner to create the design in Fig. 5-46. The scanner copied my signature and sewed it combined with a programmed flower design. (I want one of these!)

Using the Pfaff 7550 manual programmer gives a clear idea of how this works. You draw the design you want (greatly enlarged) on graphed programmer sheets, then trace your design in a continuous line, punching in stitch points (needle insertions) as you draw. For zigzag stitching, you would draw a zigzag line of points.

You need to draw in logical sequence, since the machine follows your line. Program the completed design into the machine memory and it will sew your design.

Manually programming your own stitches is a task for patient people, but computer software can make this quicker and easier. You can create a design on the computer screen and program this into your machine directly or by disk with certain machines. Again you program point-by-point needle insertions, but you can speed this up with automatic fill-in commands. You can also customize the machine's built-in stitches.

When Ron Abraham, owner and expert repairman at Universal Sew and Vac, where I take my machines, recently returned from the national conventions, he related with great enthusiasm the wonders of new model sewing machines. Most now have automated sewing hoops for accuracy and ease of sewing. I can hardly wait to see them all!

5-46. My signature scanned into the New Home Memory Craft 8000 and sewn automatically with a programmed flower design. Sewn by Ron Abraham.

ABCDEFGH
IJKLMNOP
QRSTUVW
XYZ   abc
defghijklmno
pqrstuvwxyz

*5-47. Chancery Zapf Alphabet. You can use this italic alphabet
to copy and adapt for a wide variety of projects.*

6-1. Circle monograms, popular earlier in this century, are back in style. They can be appliquéd directly on your towels or on a background fabric first. Use washable fabrics. Photo by Donna H. Chiarelli.

CHAPTER SIX

Monograms

Many animals mark their turf, to say "This is Mine!" but humans have raised this activity to a high art through monograms. Monograms are initials arranged into a design and applied to possessions. They are a terrific way to personalize a wide variety of items through stitchery. A look at gift catalogs these days shows that you can monogram anything from turtlenecks to towels, bags to belts, pillows to pajamas, shirts to shoes, bibs to blankets, hats to handkerchiefs, and picture frames to pet clothes. Personalizing a gift with a monogram makes it special. And monogramming personal items of college students or travelers is a good means of identification. You can even start a small home business doing monograms.

Traditionally, monograms have been embroidered by hand onto fabric objects, but they can also be carved into wooden furniture,

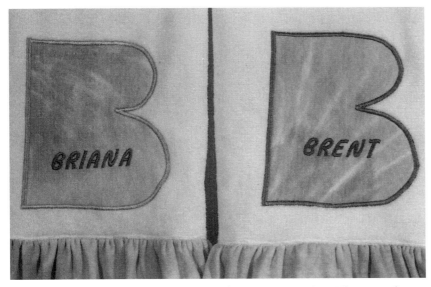

6-2. You can use a wide variety of styles for monogramming. These towels feature a combination of automatic embroidery and appliqué. Note that the lettering is positioned so it shows (right-side-up) when hung on a towel bar.

6-3. Some sewing machines not only have monogram-style letters, but wreathes, shields and other decorative elements to surround the letter. This Old English monogram was sewn on a Brother 7000.

stamped into brass plaques, engraved into silverware, etched or sandblasted into glass doors, tooled into leather saddles, or painted onto many surfaces.

This chapter features machine appliqué monograms, but you can create them using any number of sewing techniques—from machine-sewn monograms to hand-sewn cross-stitch, crewel, and satin-stitch, to name a few. Throughout this book you'll find information on a wide variety of techniques you can use to create them, including machine embroidery, programmed machine embroidery, trapunto, or even fabric paint. You also can use any alphabet typeface for monogramming, and you'll find many to try in this book as well. Try a traditional monogram style, or create your own.

When you plan a monogram, keep in mind that embroidered monograms show up best on finely textured, plain-colored fabrics. They look rich on lustrous satin, texture-woven damask, or dense-pile velveteen, terry cloth, or velour. With print fabrics or multicolored weaves, you'll have to experiment to see what succeeds. Increasing the color contrast or the size of the monogram makes it more visible.

Once you have settled on a technique, you'll need to decide which initials to use, and where to put them. Here are some guidelines to help you.

Whose Initials?

First off, it helps to get the terminology straight: a given name is a person's first name, such as Patricia; a surname is their last, family, or married name, such as Hall; a maiden name is a woman's surname before marriage. Over

6-4. In a monogram with three letters all the same size, the last letter is the first letter of your surname. With letters of different sizes, the largest one is the surname.

time, monogramming has been codified into formal etiquette, which decrees whose initials were used as monograms and what the lettering style could be. Today, customs are changing to include hyphenated maiden and married names for women. There's also a shift to less formal address, such as Randy and Pat rather than Mr. and Mrs. Randall R. Hall. As a result, few of these rules remain, but there are some customs you may want to maintain. The customs of the moment are as follows:

❖ In a group of three initials of the same size, the last letter is your surname's first letter. With three initials of different sizes, the largest is the surname (see Fig. 6-4).

❖ A man's personal item with one letter shows the first letter of his surname; on a woman's, the first letter of her first name appears. (This because women

usually take the husband's last name.)

❖ On household items, use the single initial of the last name, but on bed and bath linens, use the first and last initials, or all three initials, of the person using them.

❖ Married women and brides-to-be often monogrammed household linens with three initials: their first name initial, their maiden surname initial, and their married surname initial.

With the changing custom on names, it's easy to see why monogramming styles have changed as well. You may choose to be tasteful and correct, as stated above, or go with today's more relaxed style: use your entire first name or a nickname. Apply the popular standby "His" and "Hers" or "Mine," "Yours," and "Ours." You can even stick on a playful mes-

6-5. Place monograms in logical places where they can be seen to advantage on linens, clothing, and other possessions.

sage like "Don't touch" or "Property of _____," even emblazon an item with your school emblem, or use nonsense lettering with lots of swashes that looks impressive.

Where Does the Monogram Go?

There are also traditional locations for monograms. Here is a rundown on the basic guide lines:

❖ Towels are monogrammed above the hem or woven band and centered, so they will be visible when folded into thirds and hung over the rack.

❖ For napkins, fold as you would to use them, and monogram on the top, angled across the corner or centered along one side.

❖ Monogram tablecloths near the hem across one corner or at the host or hostess's place.

❖ For robes, pajamas, jackets, or shirts, monogram on the left breast pocket or in the pocket area. Or monogram on the top of the left shirt cuff.

❖ Put coat monograms on the lining right side, about one-third of the way up from the hem. Or for visibility, put them in the center back neck lining.

❖ Monogram turtlenecks or sweaters on the center front collar, left breast pocket area, left shoulder, across the chest, on the cuff, or wherever strikes your fancy.

❖ For bedding, apply letters so the monogram is right-side-up from the foot of the bed when the bed is made. This applies for most other objects as well, since people prefer easy reading.

Don't worry if you monogram something in a novel place. I held up a dress, said to myself "left breast pocket," shook my left hand to be sure I knew which was which, and then managed to monogram the right side—which was left when facing me. If something like this happens, just say you are starting a new custom.

Designing Monograms

Not only do monograms identify, but they serve as a design element. The letters can march sedately in a

6-6. *This script monogram is sewn in trapunto. It was created by stitching through the face of the fabric, in this case leather, which was placed over a filler like fiberfill and lining fabric for a dimensional effect.*

row, or be arranged in a variety of other shapes. The project monogram shows block letters in a circle typical of the 1920s. Some letters simply won't work with this circle concept.

You can use other shapes to contain monogram letters—consider diamonds, squares, or rectangles, or try free-form shapes. To make your monograms readable and create a balanced-looking design, certain elements gen-

erally should remain consistent: try to keep the width of letters consistent, keep them at a consistent angle (upright or slanted to the same degree), and use a consistent typeface or style of letter. Of course, you can experiment with breaking any of these rules for innovative effect, but start with the above parameters.

It's fun to mesh decorative and script letters together into rhythmic designs. To try this, use tracing

paper over a fancy typeface. Trace one of the letters, lay this tracing over the next and see how they mesh. You can lengthen swashes, change angles slightly or shift the letters up or down (as a rule, keep them upright). Add a few more furbelows as needed to complete the overall design. (See Fig. 6-6 for an example I created with my own initials and Fig 6-7 for examples of designs you can create.) Then try the technique yourself using the type in Fig. 6-8.

6-7. *To experiment with designing monograms, trace script letters (or any other alphabet) and then try different ideas for combining, overlapping, and intertwining them into a design. Then add decorative touches like frames or borders.*

ABCDE
FGHIJK
LMNOPQ
RSTUVW
XYZ

abdefghijklmnop
qrstuvwxyz
1234567890

6-8. Bankenscript Alphabet. This alphabet has rhythmic, thick-and-thin letters that slant even more than italic ones do. They have decorative swashes and added ball finishing touches for even more elegant effect.

MONOGRAMMED TOWELS

6-9. Letters can be appliquéd directly on the towels or onto a background fabric. These examples were sewn on a Viking 300 computerized sewing machine with Janome/New Home embroidery threads on metallic and satin fabrics.

Overview. This project explains how to embroider and appliqué large letters on ready-made towels, both with and without a contrasting background fabric for the monogram. You can adapt the directions to add monograms to other personal items as well. To create a monogram, select the letters you need, scale them to size, choose colors and fabrics, and sew some beautiful towels.

Technique. Monograms are designed into a large circle. They are appliquéd and satin-stitched by machine onto ready-made towels using one or more layers of appliqué fabric. The lettering was traced on tracing paper to make the pattern, then sewn through it to transfer. You can hand satin stitch these letters if you prefer.

Type style. Circle Monogram is an art deco style typeface. All three letters fit into a circle (see Fig. 6-10 on facing page). Diamond Monogram, shown in Fig. 6-12 on facing page, is a variation.

Size. Materials given below will create a 6" (15cm) diameter monogram, which looks attractive on both a standard-size bath towel and a hand towel. Use any size towel you prefer, and size the monogram accordingly. Buy washcloths to practice on; they're inexpensive and are good for experimenting with colors and fabrics.

Color concept. You can select the towel and coordinate the monogram fabrics around that, or start with fabrics you would like to work with and select a towel that will complement them.

Design the Monogram

1. To make the pattern guide, enlarge the circle pattern in Fig. 6-13, page 84, to 6" (15cm) in diameter or any size you wish. Using a photocopy machine, scale up the pattern on graph paper, or use a compass to duplicate it. Use your drafting tools (ruler, compass, triangle, T-square, S-curve) and a sharp pencil to trace the lines of the emblem for an accurate pattern. The vertical and horizontal

MATERIALS AND SUPPLIES

Base fabric. Ready-made terry cloth or velour towel.

Appliqué fabrics. 8" (20.5cm) square of each color.

Recommended fabrics. Terry cloth, velour, linen, heavy cotton, fleece or the like. Use ready-made towels, robes, tote bags, or make your own. Be sure all fabric you use is washable.

Threads. Thread that matches the towel as well as contrasting or color-keyed machine embroidery thread that will go with your appliqué fabrics.

Tools and supplies. For drafting the pattern: tracing paper, pencil, ruler, and tape, and a compass, T-square, triangle, and/or S-curve. For sewing the monogram: sharp scissors, appliqué scissors, fusible backing, tearaway backing or backing paper (scrap typing paper is fine), quilting pins (1½" [4cm]), zigzag sewing machine.

lines within this indicate letter widths, ½" (1.3cm).

2. Select your monogram letters from Fig. 6-10. Note that your letters will vary in shape according to position in the circle. (The same would hold true for a diamond, ellipse, or free-form shape.) For example the "A" curves one way in the first or left-hand circle position, is equal-sided in the center, and curves the other way on the right. Some letters don't "read" well in certain positions—the "Q" and "L" are missing altogether in one position. Use a diamond-shape monogram (Fig. 6-12) or script letters instead if you don't like the way the letters look.

3. Lay tracing paper over the circle diagram and use the lines needed within the circle to trace your letters onto tracing paper (see Fig. 6-11). Use a scale rule and S-curve to make mechanically

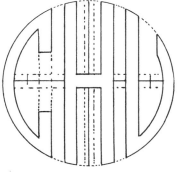

6-11. To make your pattern, use tracing paper over your enlarged (or reduced) circle pattern (Fig. 6-13). Draw in your initials using the guide lines, making all strokes the same width. Use drafting tools for accuracy.

6-10. Circle Block Alphabet. This alphabet features block letters—all the strokes are the same width—distorted to fit into a circle.

6-12. Diamond Block Alphabet. The letters in this alphabet are similar to Circle Block ones, with all strokes the same width, but they are distorted to fit into a diamond shape instead.

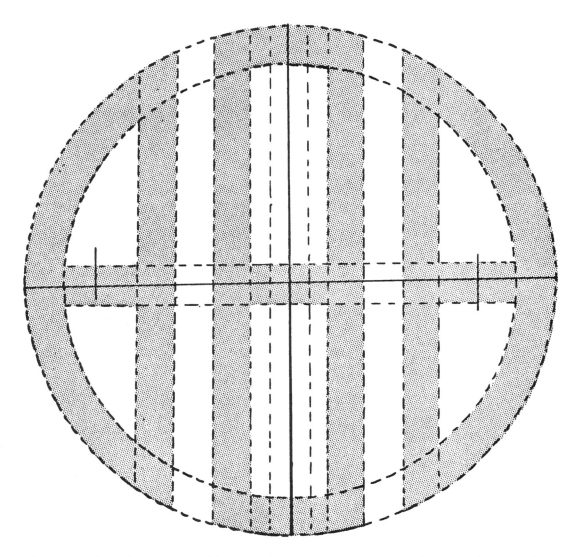

6-13. Use this pattern for making circle block letters. Enlarge to size, and use the guide lines to draw your letters.

smooth lines. This pattern will be ruined as a stitching guide during sewing, so make additional patterns for each towel.

Appliqué the Design

1. Using the fabric you plan to use to sew your monogram (I used a multicolored metallic fabric), cut out a circle slightly larger than 6" (15cm).

2. Iron on fusible backing to stabilize the fabric. (Use a low-temperature fusible backing for metallic fabric.) Remove the backing paper.

3. Place the paper monogram pattern on the face-up appliqué fabric. Pin it on the towel, centered, and 4" (10 cm) up from the hem. Or place as you wish depending on the towel size and hem style.

4. Pin tear-away backing on the reverse side of the towel, behind the monogram, so it extends beyond the monogram stitching line, to stabilize it and help it feed evenly.

5. Use thread that matches the towel for the bobbin, and a contrasting or color-keyed machine

embroidery thread on the top. Using a narrow zigzag stitch, sew around each letter through the tracing paper, using it as a guide. You'll satin-stitch over this line to give a finished look later.

6. Tear off the tracing paper pattern. Use the closed tips of your scissors to score a line in the paper for easier tearing. It pays to work over a wastebasket for this step, since it gets messy. Leave the backing stabilizer in place. Cut away fabric from around the letters using appliqué or sewing scissors (or a razor blade on velour towels). Press the fused-fabric letters; use limited heat if they're sewn with metallic fabric.

7. To sew the satin-stitching that covers the trimmed edges and the zigzag stitching line, align the needle so it sews into the appliqué fabric on one side, and covers the trimmed edge on the other (see Fig. 6-14). Satin-stitch around each letter, sewing the letter's interior lines first and finishing with the outside circle to complete the monogram. Sew a second line of satin-stitching over the first for best coverage.

8. Clip threads and then remove backing paper by scoring with the closed tips of your scissors to facilitate tearing (see Fig. 6-15).

Monogramming with Background Fabric

To create a monogram with contrasting background fabric, follow the steps below:

1. Cut out a circle slightly larger than 6" (15cm) for both the background fabric and the letter fabric.

2. Trace the monogram pattern in reverse on fusible backing and iron this on the back of the lettering fabric.

3. Cut out the letters, remove the backing paper, and use the pattern to align the letters on the background circle. Pin or tape them in place. Iron the letters onto the background fabric.

4. Position the pattern, letter fabric, and background fabric in place on your towel (see placement guide lines in step 3, page 84). To complete the monogram, follow Steps 4 through 8 on pages 84–85.

Monogramming with Decorative Stitches and Background Fabric

You can also combine decorative stitching with monograms. Here's how I created the circle and diamond monogram shown in Fig. 6-16.

1. Cut out a circle slightly larger than 6" for the background fabric. Then cut out the diamond shape, $\frac{1}{4}$" (6mm) all around larger than needed. (The finished diamond on the towel I made is $4\frac{3}{4}$" [12cm] on all sides, which means it was cut to $5\frac{1}{4}$" [13cm].)

2. Iron fusible backing onto the circle fabric. Cut out the circle shape, remove backing paper, and iron the circle onto the diamond shape. Iron fusible backing on the back of the diamond back for increased stability.

3. Trace the letters on the circle in removable markings such as tailor's chalk.

4. Set your machine to the pattern stitch you want, and sew the letters.

5. Remove the diamond backing paper, turn under $\frac{1}{4}$" (6mm) hems all around, and iron the diamond, with circle and letters, onto the towel. Add backing paper to the back of the towel.

6. Satin-stitch around the circle. Decorative stitch around the diamond. Add other decorative stitching as desired.

6-14. To make strong finished edges, satin-stitch over the trimmed basting. Pivot on corners to overlap or meet previous stitching so no gaps appear in the satin-stitched outline.

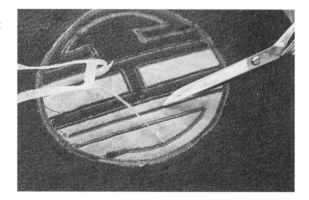

6-15. After satin-stitching the monogram, score the paper backing with the tips of your scissors to facilitate removal.

6-16. There are lots of ways to vary and embellish monograms. This example shows a decorative-stitching monogram sewn on a decorative fabric.

7-1. Labels can be as simple or as elaborate and inventive as the creations they adorn. You can letter them by hand using cross-stitch, hand embroidery, or permanent pen. You can also make attractive labels with both conventional sewing machines and the new computerized models. Photo by Donna H. Chiarelli.

CHAPTER SEVEN

Labels by Hand and Machine

For most artists, it is the pleasure of creating that matters more than the credit, but labels do have practical uses. They not only record who made a particular piece, but they can also record when it was created and any other important facts about the piece—its title or a dedication, for example. They can even record a piece of history: signed blocks on autograph quilts, popular in the 1840s, may now be the only trace of women of that era, who were then not listed on the census roles. Early clothing manufacturers recognized the value of labels and added them to their clothing as advertising. For a time, coat-neck labels were sewn in upside down so they could be read as the coat hung over a church pew. Now manufacturers are not so subtle; their labels appear on the outside of cloth-

ing—the bigger the better.

You can use almost any technique in this book to create labels for your projects. This chapter provides an overview of them and includes ideas for stitches to use and designs to try.

Planning and Making Labels

Some stitchers plan the label from the beginning, as part of the project—a quilt block design, for example. Others add the signature later on a sewn-on patch. Quilters label their works sometimes to

show pride of accomplishment, other times to identify the work when shown or to send a message. Sue Holdaway-Heys, who is earning her master's degree at the University of Michigan, uses quilting as her art form. It hasn't been easy for academia to take this cozy medium seriously. Her labels list name, address, title, size, and sometimes the label provided for a certain exhibition. She uses indelible ink on her labels.

Many common hand embroidery stitches can be used to embroider names. Art quilter Mary Gentry hand embroiders her name using bullion stitching for greater

7-2. Bullion-stitch letters stand out clearly because of the thick "strokes" created by the wrapped stitches.

7-3. Cross-stitch fabric provides a graph for making orderly letters. Sue Vosburg Scherado cross-stitched this label for an ABC quilt designed by her sister, Mary Zee, and sewed by her father.

bulk (see Fig. 7-2 on previous page). She signs machine-sewn quilts by free-motion machine stitching. Suzanne Scherado cross-stitched the label and used it as one of the quilt blocks on a cherished family quilt (see Fig. 7-3). See Chapter 9 for information on graphing letters, which is an ideal technique for creating cross-stitch or crewel labels.

Nancy Meyer sews entire messages on her quilt backs with automatic stitches on her Pfaff sewing machine. I used a Brother PC 7000 on my self portrait done for a group painting show to label everything in it as the concept of the artwork (see Fig. 1-1).

Labelmaking Guidelines

Use the following guidelines to help you find your own style of labels.

❖ Make your label consistent with the stitchery. Don't sign an elegant stitchery with a crude signature. See Fig. 7-5 for a sampling of the stitches you can use to sign your pieces.

❖ Be aware of requirements. Some quilt shows do not allow

the artist's signature to show, and require that labels that do show be covered with a sewn-on patch.

❖ Consider function. Who hasn't had a neck label that itched unbearably? Be careful of using monofilament or metallic threads on clothing for this reason.

❖ Make sure the label is washable if the stitchery will be washed; permanent if it will be dry-cleaned.

❖ Think about placement. Some labels you want immediately visible so you can locate the object; on others the label should be obscured inside. Be careful of labeling children's clothing outside where the name might be misappropriated.

Signatures

The easiest and most authentic way to sign a piece is to use a signature written in pen. To make a label this way on fabric, you must use permanent ink that is compatible with the fabric. Permanent-ink pens and the texture of fabric may impede signing a free-flowing signature. It's a good idea to practice on a scrap of fabric before you sign the real piece to get the feel of how these pens work.

If you plan to hand embroider a signature, make (or request) larger-than-normal hand-

writing to compensate for the thread thickness. To machine embroider a signature, place the signed paper over the fabric, pin in place, and stitch through it (see Fig. 7-4). Tear off the paper and pick out any paper bits with tweezers. You can also sew labels with the small-sized lettering on automated sewing machines.

1. Plan the label message on paper. Spell everything correctly and make sure the date is right. Then plan the layout so you will know where to start sewing. Use symmetrical balance, with words and phrases balanced on a center line, as in the example shown in Fig. 7-6. Or try an asymmetrical design, with an even border on the left, or design a label with random placement—whatever appeals to you.

2. Sew the label on uncut fabric so it can be held taut in an embroidery hoop. Use backing or tear-away stabilizer on the back if necessary. For small labels (such as ones sewn on ribbons) baste them onto a larger piece of fabric to embroider, then remove and sew in place. This helps to control the label while you sew and lets you stretch them tight in the embroidery hoop.

3. Draw chalk guide lines, or sew them with long basting stitches.

4. Stretch the fabric taut in the embroidery hoop, put it in the machine, and either program the stitches you want or hand-guide

7-4. To sew your signature, write it large enough to sew on paper, pin the paper to fabric, and free-motion straight-stitch through the paper. Tear away the perforated paper.

Backstitch

**Buttonhole or
Appliqué Stitch**

Feather Stitch

Running Chain Stitch

Satin-Stitch

Double Feather Stitch

Ladder Stitch

Lazy Daisy Stitch

Straight-Stitch

French Knot

Bullion Stitch

*7-5. All of these stitches can be used to create and decorate labels.
The bullion stitch, lower right, is made like a French knot: twist the
thread around the needle, pull the thread through, and then sew into
fabric at the end of the bullion.*

MACHINE-SEWN LABELS

Overview. Most labels and badges are small in size, with small lettering. The label can be a simple signature or an elaborate decorative design.

Technique. This example was sewn by automatic machine embroidery, but labels can be sewn by hand as well.

Type style. Italic, shadow, script, roman, or continuous block. See Fig. 7-7 for suitable typefaces to use.

Color concept. Colors can blend to diminish the label's visibility, harmonize as a decorative accent, or contrast for immediate recognition.

7-6. I used the Brother 7000 sewing machine and lettering disc to embroider this label for the Mother Goose Quilt.

the machine as it sews.

5. Finish the label edges with a hem, or with serging or overcasting stitches (see Fig. 7-8). Sew it in place or use an iron-on fuser to adhere the label in place.

7-8. You can machine sew, embroider, or print label information onto pieces of ribbon or fabric, fold the edges under, and sew the label in place. Suit the label design, size, and information you include to the object you have created.

A B C D E F G H I J K L M N O P
Q R S T U V W X Y Z
a b c d e f g h i j k l m n o p q r s t
u v w x y z   1 2 3 4 5 6 7 8 9 0

A B C D E F G H I J K L M
N O P Q R S T U V W X Y Z
a b c d e f g h i j k l m
n o p q r s t u v w x y z
1 2 3 4 5 6 7 8 9 0

A B C D E F G H I J K L M N O P Q
R S T U V W X Y Z
d b c d e f g h i j k l m n o p q r s
t u v w x y z   1 2 3 4 5 6 7 8 9 0

A B C D E F G H I J K L M N O
P Q R S T U V W X Y Z
a b c d e f g h i j k l m n o p q r s t u v
w x y z   1 2 3 4 5 6 7 8 9

7-7. Label Typefaces Alphabet. This provides some suitable type styles for lettering a label. From the top they are Palatino italic, Courier (typewriter style), hand printing, hand writing (cursive).

MATERIALS AND SUPPLIES

Recommended fabrics. Firmly woven fabrics, poly-cotton, satin ribbon, even-weave cross-stitch fabric. Suit the fabric or materials to the piece.

Fabric amounts. To machine-sew labels, start with a fabric large enough to fit the hoop on your machine (or your embroidery hoop, if you hand-guide the fabric). Trim after sewing to the desired size.

Threads. Thread in colors complementing your project.

Tools and supplies. Paper, pencils, backing or tear-away stabilizer, chalk, scissors, sewing machine.

CHAPTER EIGHT

Hand Lettering with Your Sewing Machine

Yes, those top-of-the-line computer sewing machines make the best embroidered lettering. But what if you don't have one? Well, if you don't have a typewriter or word processor, you fall back on handwriting. You can do the same on your sewing machine, by using your handwriting to embroider lettering. In this chapter you'll learn just how to do it.

To create free-motion style lettering on a sewing machine, it helps to imagine the needle as a pen held upright in place. In this case, though, to write, you must move the surface (your fabric) under the stationary pen (the

needle). You can write by free-motion embroidery directly on the fabric if a casual effect is called for. Just trace or write the letters on the fabric first with erasable markings, such as tailor's chalk pencil. Or write out the message on a tracing paper pattern of the object and sew through this. Before creating a design to sew, practice using the free-motion technique to develop an even flow.

Adjust Your Machine

The first step is to adjust your machine. One way or another, nearly every sewing machine can

sew free-motion, including the old straight-stitch foot pedal ones. You simply need to make the right adjustments. When you make adjustments on your machine, the aim is twofold: to eliminate the motion of the feed dogs (those little serrated prongs sticking up through the machine needle plate that move the fabric along, see Fig. 8-1) and to diminish or eliminate the pressure of the presser foot. Remember you, not the feed dogs, will be moving the fabric.

Read your sewing machine manual to see if you can lower the feed dogs. Set them to the shortest stitch length possible if you cannot. For stitches to form, the

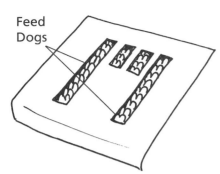

8-1. Feed dogs move fabric along while you guide it through the machine. In order to sew free-motion lettering, you need to lower the position of the feed dogs.

presser bar lever must be down to engage the thread tension and to keep the fabric on the needle plate. Consult your manual again to see if you can alter the presser foot pressure, usually with a dial on the left end. If you can't, check your accessory box for an embroidery foot. The foot part will be a small metal or plastic hoop or a metal spring. This device must maintain pressure on the fabric while the needle is down (looping the bobbin to form the stitch) but ease off when up so you can move the fabric freely by hand.

Become a Hoop

You will be using your hands as a sewing hoop to form the letters. If your fabric is large enough, you can put it in a sewing machine embroidery hoop and guide it with your hands on each side. (For this reason, it's a good idea to cut fabric to size after you embroider it.) Or guide the fabric by placing your hands on both sides of it like an embroidery hoop. (Practice on scrap fabric first! It takes a while to coordinate hand and machine speeds.) To keep the fabric taut, try gripping

the fabric on each side in your fists to move the fabric more freely.

Unless you are working on a very stiff fabric you will need a stabilizing material on the back of the fabric. Otherwise, straight or zigzag free-motion stitches will pull in and pucker the fabric. For best results, fuse on another fabric, use tearaway backing, or do both.

8-2. With free-motion embroidery, you use your hands to guide the fabric.

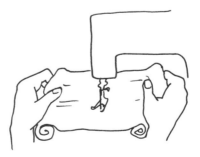

8-3. To keep the fabric taut, either use an embroidery hoop, or use your hands as a hoop. Pulling the rolled-up ends of the fabric taut as you sew is also effective.

Making Letters

For free-motion sewing, run the machine at a fairly fast speed to avoid trying to move the fabric while the needle is down—this can result in a broken needle and may throw the machine timing off. But don't build up such a pile of stitches that you can't advance. With the machine going fast, slowly and smoothly move the fabric with both hands to trace the letters.

Straight-Stitch Letters

Try straight-stitch free-motion sewing first. Set the machine to the shortest stitch length, so the feed dogs won't move. Set the presser foot pressure so it is very low, or use an embroidery foot. (Some newer machines aim to sew in four directions or more using the feed dogs to eliminate the need to turn the fabric, but this is not fluid enough for writing.) To experiment, try signing your name or making a big outline letter in stitches on practice fabric.

With straight-stitch free-motion you need to pretend you are a colored pencil. To get a broad stroke you must make many small ones. Moving the fabric continuously forward in small circles is easier than back and forth. Try various fill-in patterns for effect.

Zigzag Letters

For satin-stitch letters, set the sewing machine to medium zigzag (2.5 mm width) with a very short stitch length (.2 or .3). To sew zigzag letters, you need not turn the fabric as you sew. Pretend you are a robot that can only move the fabric up, down, and sideways with both hands firmly in place. (Notice that the zigzag stitches are all horizontal in Fig. 8-5.) Vertical zigzagging looks fine once you

8-4. Straight-stitch free-motion sewing forms words on fabric almost as easily as writing with a pen, as shown on this wedding quilt square created for Dave and Tori Goodrich.

8-6. You can even sew Old English printing by zigzag free-motion stitching.

8-5. For zigzag free-motion stitching, you need to maintain the same angle of stitching without turning the fabric.

develop an even rhythm, but going sideways the stitches sew into each other. To diminish this effect, angle the fabric to the left before you begin. If you want an up-and-down stitch, angle the fabric side-ways, but always use both hands to keep from turning the fabric while sewing. Once you are used to this, it's much easier than constant turning.

The Old English stitching sample (Fig. 8-6) shows how to take advantage of the sideways stitching effect of zigzag free-motion. Vertical strokes turn out wide and cross strokes light, the same effect you would get from a calligraphy pen with a wide or flexible point. Practice with a calligraphy pen or a chisel-shaped marker to see how your letters will turn out.

Make a Pattern

Now that you have tested your handwriting to see how it spaces out and practiced free-motion sewing, plan your design. How will you arrange the lettering to achieve the effect you want? Sketch your idea on paper to develop your ideas. (It's easier to edit ideas on paper than in your mind.) Make a full-size paper pattern so you can fit the lettering in place. Then have some fun expressing yourself!

What to Make?

How about a gift? Handmade gifts give extended pleasure. As you make them, you imagine how this gift will be enjoyed. My granddaughter wouldn't wear the dress I made her—it itched, she rightly said—but helping her choose that magenta metallic fabric was worth the effort. While stitching on it, I had envisioned her sparkling more adorably than Shirley Temple, even though in fact she wears her baseball cap backwards. Even so, she shares my delight in fabrics and the possibilities.

My great affection for fabrics came from my mother, with whom I've roamed many a fabric store aisle. "There's a Cloth World only two blocks away," she reported with pleasure when she moved to Florida. She never could find her mislaid glasses down there, so I made her a bright-colored googley-eyed case decorated with free-motion embroidery that helped solve the problem. It's the first project for this chapter.

The second project is a wedding photo album made for my new daughter-in-law and our son. It, too, features free-motion embroidery, but it also uses a photo-transfer technique that I think you will enjoy experimenting with. Both projects make great gifts.

MOM'S GLASSES CASE

8-7. Looking For These? Glasses Case, a gift made for Mom who never could find her glasses. The embroidery was done on a machine using the free-motion technique.

Overview. This small gift takes little material and not much time to construct. The base fabric is felt with lettering applied by free-motion machine embroidery. The googley eyes, available in craft stores, are glued on.

Technique. Free-motion zigzag machine embroidery with the fabric guided by hand as described above.

Type style. Handwriting, or cursive script, see Fig. 8-8.

Size. 3½" X 7½" (9cm X 19.5cm).

8-8. Free-Motion Cursive Alphabet. Use these letters as a guide for handwritten free-motion lettering. Or use your own handwriting style. The width of the zigzag will affect the size of the letter, so narrow the zigzag setting for smaller lettering.

ABCDEFG
HIJKLMN
OPQRSTU
VWXYZ &
abcdefghi
jklmnopqr
stuvwxyz

Cut Out the Fabric

1. Trace or scale up the pattern (see Fig. 8-9), then pin or mark it on the fabrics.

2. Cut out the three layers and the stabilizer backing.

3. Trace the design on the top fabric with white tailor's chalk pencil or other removable marking device. Or draw the design on

---

MATERIALS AND SUPPLIES

Note that the dimensions below include seam allowances.

Outer layer fabric. Blue felt 8" X 8½" (20.5cm X 22cm).

Inner layer(s) fabric. Heavy fabric or interfacing 8" X 8½" (20.5cm X 22cm).

Lining. Orange felt 8" X 8½" (20.5cm X 22cm).

Recommended fabrics. Two layers of felt over an inner layer of heavy fabric, which acts as a stabilizer for machine embroidery and firms up the case. The outside layer could be made from an assortment of fabrics including denim, Ultrasuede, velveteen, or others.

Backing. Tear-away stabilizer 4" X 8½" (10cm X 11cm).

Tools and supplies. Zigzag sewing machine, metallic thread (Sulky copper color 142 7011), white embroidery thread, blue sewing thread, sharp scissors, and two ¾" (2cm) googley eyes, available at craft stores. If you can't find them, appliqué fabric eyes in place.

8-9. Glasses Case Pattern. For fabrics that fray, add ½" (1.3cm) seam allowance for turning edges.

tracing paper and use this on top as a sewing guide.

4. To assemble the layers, pin the outer layer to the inner layer, keeping the pins outside the sewing area. Pin or tape the backing paper or tear-away stabilizer on the back of the design area, again keeping pins outside the stitching lines. Draw or pin the design on the top, making sure to carefully align it.

Embroider the Design

1. Set your machine for medium-width (2.5mm) zigzag satin-stitch.

2. Thread the machine with white embroidery thread for the wording, bronze metallic thread for the glasses. Or use colors you select.

3. Sew the design as shown in Fig. 8-10 and described in the beginning of this chapter. If free-motion simply doesn't work for you, set the machine for zigzag satin-stitch and sew normally, guiding the fabric along with the feed dogs. Tear away the stabilizer.

4. Steam press the design flat. This technique tends to pucker the fabric.

Assemble the Glasses Case

The way you assemble the case depends on whether you are using a fabric that will fray or not. For a fabric that will fray, add ½" (1.3cm) seam allowance. Stack the lining fabric face down on the embroidered layers and align the edges. Sew around the case with ½" (1.3cm) seam allowance, leaving a 2" (5cm) opening on the bottom edge to turn. Trim the seam allowance, turn, tuck in the opening edges and press.

For a non-fraying fabric such as felt, Ultrasuede or leather, stack the three layers in finished order; upper, inner and under (see Fig 8-11). For the turned edge, beginning at the curved edge, topstitch with matching thread across the top of the case. Clip the threads. For the non-fray edge, topstitch and then trim the edges close to

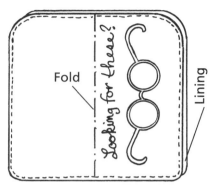

8-11. Add the lining to the case by seaming the layers and turning the case. Or topstitch the layers together and trim.

the stitch line with sharp scissors.

Fold the case vertically to align both sides, and continue the stitch line, back-stitching at the end to secure (see Fig. 8-12). This topstitching will also sew the turned opening closed.

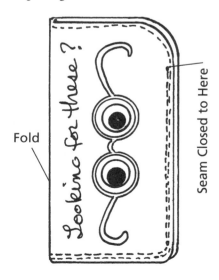

8-12. To complete the case, fold it in half and topstitch to join the edges.

8-10 For accurate stitching, pin a tracing paper pattern on top of the case and sew through it to make the lettering and the design.

GIFT ALBUM

8-13. What better way to personalize a gift than with a photograph and the names of the recipients?

Overview. This project shows you how to personalize an album cover with lettering as well as a wedding picture, child's picture, or the event invitation. Lettering can be part of the photo or can be machine-embroidered.

Technique. Free-motion machine embroidery, book covering, and photo gel transfer, which allows you to move an image from its paper backing to a fabric one.

Type style. Free-motion satin-stitch cursive writing.

Sizes. Commercial album 7½" X 10" X 2" (19.5cm X 25.5cm X 5cm).

Color concept. The eggshell colored base fabric tended to mute the photograph colors to a mellow hue. You can transfer an image onto any color fabric—with mixed results, some amazing, some awful.

Using Photo Transfer

Photo transfer is a fascinating way to create imagery on fabric. There are several ways to transfer images to fabric photographically, including screen printing, blueprinting, and using fabric treated with light-sensitive photo emulsion (see Fig. 8-14 on page 98). Craft stores will have information on these techniques.

Probably the easiest technique is photo transfer. In this process, a transfer gel is applied to a photograph, photocopy, or printed

MATERIALS AND SUPPLIES

Fabric cover. 10" X 28" (25.5cm X 71cm) white or eggshell poly-cotton

End papers. 10" X 14" (25.5cm X 35.5cm) matching paper or use any color you like

Recommended fabrics. Cotton, poly-cotton, canvas or other firmly woven, light-colored fabric.

Threads. Blue-green or harmonizing rayon machine embroidery thread.

Tools and supplies. A ready-made white photo album, a sewing machine that can sew free-motion, scissors, ink roller (brayer), plastic tray or newspapers, wax paper, paper towel, rotary cutter, metal ruler, glue stick, sponge, and fabric-to-plastic glue—white glue, Tacky Glue, Goop, or contact glue.

Photo transfer supplies. Photograph or other image, jar or bottle of Picture This Transfer Medium or acrylic medium.

8-14. Isolde deVries used photographic negatives to project images on light-sensitive fabric to create blueprint fabric imagery and lettering for her quilt.

page. This gel, called Picture This Transfer Medium, or acrylic paint medium, adheres to the printing ink or photographic emulsion. Additional coatings of the gel toughen this layer into a plastic sheet of gel. The backing is removed and the image applied to fabric.

Lettering can compose part or all of the imagery on the photocopy. Just select print from magazines or draw your own lettering and photocopy it. Or the printing can be embroidered onto the transferred image as shown in the project.

Selecting an Image

The transfer gel works best on black-and-white photos (if they are paper-backed) and printed text. For color images, take your photo to a color photocopy machine and enlarge it to size. The gel tends to dissolve the red ink from colored photocopies, causing a pink hue to the finished piece. If you use a colored photograph, ask the printer at the copy shop to diminish the amount of

red in the copy. The red returns with the gel.

A small photo can be enlarged to double the size, but you may be limited by the copier's paper size. Some copiers (Xerox) will make color copies from slides. Some copiers can reverse the image onto paper or acetate. This way you can coat it and transfer directly to the fabric. The acetate makes a shiny surface; the paper, a matte one.

You need less gel for this, giving a more natural finish.

Transferring the Image

1. Trim the image to size. Dilute the acrylic medium to a creamy consistency with water if needed. Lay the photocopy flat on newsprint or a kitchen tray, and paint or roll on a thin coating of gel (see Fig. 8-15). Do not re-brush or re-roll, since the colors will smear. Let it dry. Then add two more coats, letting the gel dry thoroughly between coats. (If you have an image that was reversed during the copying process, cover it with gel, place it on the prepared fabric, and roll it firmly to adhere.)

8-15

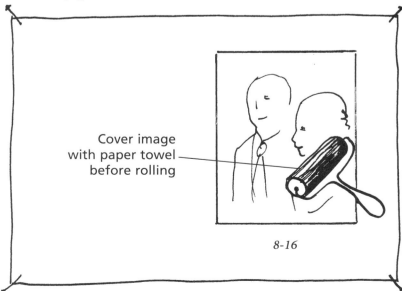

Cover image with paper towel before rolling

8-16

2. When the gel is thoroughly dry (it takes a day), turn the picture face down in a tray or on newspaper and water soak it to loosen the paper backing. Peel the backing off. Easy to say, longer to do, since the paper never comes off whole but in strips. Keep wetting the paper and rubbing gently with a soft pot scrubber to roll off remaining fibers. Work carefully until you can see the picture in reverse clearly. For a reversed photo on fabric, clean off backing paper, and you're done.

3. To prepare the fabric backing wash it first to remove any sizing. Iron it smooth. Spread the fabric and tape it down taut. Mark the image placement with pins.

4. To move the image, place it on wax paper and apply a coating of gel medium. The gel must be smooth and cover the image completely. Flip the image onto the fabric—gel down, face up—and position it within the markings. Remove the pins. Cover the image with a paper towel and roll with an ink roller (brayer) to bond the image well with the fabric (see Fig. 8-16). Coat the entire piece of fabric with gel to give a consistent surface. Both will be waterproof. Let this dry for at least a day.

Embroidering the Lettering

The gel on fabric is not tough enough for a sewing machine hoop since this may damage the image. To embroider, tape or pin a non-woven stabilizer fabric on the back of the fabric. Set your sewing machine to free-motion sewing with a medium-wide satin-stitch. Then, before you sew on the real fabric, review the techniques for free-motion sewing earlier in this chapter and sew a test strip on similar fabric.

Use your test strip as a spacing guide to draw the lettering on tracing paper. You can pin this in place to sew through, or draw a light base guide line by ruler with a tailor's chalk pencil. On gel-coated fabric, you need to embroider the names right the first time, since stitches will leave holes in the fabric. Follow your paper pattern or chalk-drawn letters to embroider the names.

Run the machine rapidly and coordinate your hands in guiding the fabric so you produce an even-coverage satin stitch. Grip the fabric firmly in your hands on each side to keep fabric taut while free-motion embroidering to resist the pull of the stitches. You can reverse direction back over the embroidered line to fill in, if need be.

Covering the Album

1. Start by assembling the materials you will need. You need fabric-to-plastic glue, a glue stick, sponge, ruler, rotary cutter, and ink roller (brayer). Test a small piece of fabric and glue on the cover to see if it will bond well. White glue does not stick to plastic very well. Goop, Tacky Glue, and other glues will be harder to work with but may give better results.

2. Lay the completed cover, with the image face down, on white newsprint or a tray. Using the ink roller (a piece of cardboard works, too), spread the glue over the entire piece of fabric.

3. Align the front cover of the album with the image and press down. Open the album so the spine presses into the glue (see Fig. 8-17). Then open it flat to press the back cover into the glue. Lift the book and smooth the fabric with the brayer to remove bubbles and bond the fabric. Smooth the fabric taut on the entire cover. Keep your hands as clean as possible. It's important to place the image on correctly and to avoid

8-17

extensive adjusting.

4. Fold the front edge over the album cover and smooth it in place. Clip across the corner to remove extra fabric. Clip at the spine as needed to fit. Fold the top and bottom edges over the cover and smooth them out. Repeat for the back cover. Clip and fold the spine hem to fit. Then let the cover dry thoroughly.

5. To add end papers for a finished look, measure the inside covers of the album. Plan to leave $\frac{1}{4}$" (6mm) border around the outside edges (see Fig. 8-18). Use a decorative wrapping paper or other quality paper and measure two pieces to size. Spread glue smoothly on the end papers (a glue stick is handy for this). Fit the end papers into place, smooth, and close the album to press them flat.

End paper overlaps fabric cover

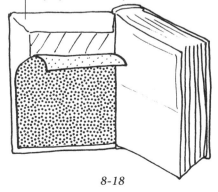

8-18

9-1. Graphing is an excellent technique for adding letters to knitted items, such as this coverlet. Knitting is also a portable craft. The ABC Knit Coverlet travelled many miles as I was making it, and has since warmed two grandchildren.

CHAPTER NINE

Graphing Letters

O ne of the easiest ways to create neat, even lettering is by charting them on graph paper. Squares on the grid correspond to fabric blocks, knit stitches, cross-stitches, or other units of construction. Charting lettering on graph paper is much like charting a brick pattern to use in building a garden wall. You can use the information in this chapter to graph and create the projects that I have designed, or design your own.

Designing Graphed Letters

To work out a design to sew or knit, you can begin directly on graph paper. It comes in various size grids in paper pads or in larger sheets you can use for bigger projects. Search for existing lettering in magazines or books for ideas and variety in lettering styles. You can lay the graph paper over this and transfer the letters into squares on the graph paper.

To combine the lettering with

a design element, lay the charted lettering over other images to see how they interweave, then transfer the best to the chart. (The cross-stitch sampler in Chapter 1 was

designed this way, with the lettering superimposed over drawings of clouds.) Keep making changes in each until the design pleases you. Some graphs come on clear

9-2. As you can see on Mary Zee's cross-stitch pillow, script letters can also be charted on a grid by stair-stepping the units.

101

plastic, so by laying this over words or a picture you can work directly without transferring. However, angled and curved lines will need translating into grid units, which take adjusting to look right. You can photocopy the transparent grid onto paper, then lay the paper over the picture and experiment with stair-stepping the curves on the grid squares until you achieve the best result. (See Fig. 9-2 on previous page, for a sample that accommodates curved letter strokes.)

Grid Size

To graph the letters of the alphabet, you will need to use a minimum of 25 squares per letter, 5 horizontal and 5 vertical, as shown in Fig. 9-3. To achieve

more detail in a graphed alphabet, increase the number of units per letter. The smaller the grid squares in relation to the letter the more detail you can achieve.

The technique you will be using to create a project will affect the size of the grid you need to use. A square grid, ideal for cross-stitch or patchwork, doesn't come out right for knitting. With knitting, the fabric itself is formed by knitting loop stitches one row into the next. The knit stitch is wider than high so there are more rows (horizontal) than stitches per square graph unit (inch or centimeter). The ratio is about five rows to three stitches, so grid squares on a knitting chart are made rectangular.

The squat "V" of a knit stitch

influences the shape of knit letters. On a large-scale knit grid, such as the ones used for the *ABC Knit Coverlet* (4 stitches to 6 rows) and the *Snug-as-a-Bug Coverlet* project with (3 units by 5 units per square inch), "Vs" in the chart show the knitted letters shapes better.

Graphing Letters and Words

Capital letters are all essentially the same height, and are easiest to graph. But because the letters are all different shapes, it is difficult to design an alphabet with letters all the same width. Putting individual letters within a framed square gives them consistency and solves this problem. Both Mary Zee's *ABC Cross-Stitch Quilt* (Fig. 9-4) and the knitted *ABC Knit Coverlet* (Fig. 9-1) are designed this way. Notice that on Mary Zee's quilt, all letters are solid, and on the *ABC Knit Coverlet* they are linear. When you graph an alphabet, make all the letter strokes consistent in thickness—even thick and thin strokes should be of consistent widths.

To graph words that are easy to read, make spaces between letters on your chart narrower than letter widths. Make spaces between words about one wide letter in width. Consistency is important, as you can see from the sample in Fig. 9-5. Spaces between lines look best if they are less than letter height.

Planning Designs

For best results, arrange the letters within the space according to some plan. Think about what effects you want to create with your lettering. For example, on the *Snug-as-a-Bug Coverlet*, the lettering is made to fit in an overall contained shape—a snug shape. This reads best by making

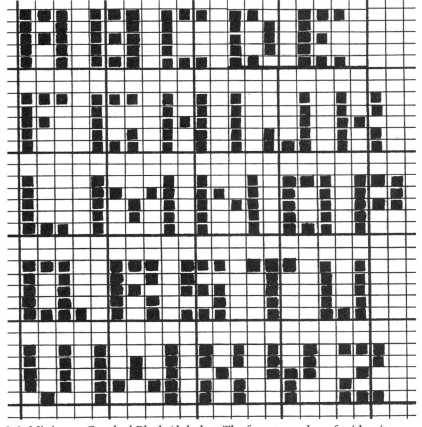

9-3. Minimum Graphed Block Alphabet. The fewest number of grid units required to make alphabet letters by graph are 25 per letter, although some need less. For more detail within each letter, use more squares.

9-4. Mary Zee's cross-stitch book, The Enchanted Alphabet, *was used to make this ABC quilt with large illustrated letters. The book is available from Mary Zee, 14809 West Point, Sterling Heights, Michigan 48078.*

Swashes
Serifs
Furbelows

Swashes
Serifs
Furbelows

9-6. *Letters can be plain or fancy, as shown by these examples. The words on top are set in plain Helvetica typeface. On the bottom, the words are the same, but the letters have been embellished with swashes, serifs, and furbelows.*

AUTOMATIC SPACING
BADS PA CI NG

9-5. *Use even spacing when you plan wording. Position letters close together and words farther apart.*

the phrases end on focal words, as do lines of poetry. Lettering in television and magazine advertisements is often made into patterns to emphasize various points or create certain effects. Sometimes the design is so strong the lettering is hard to read. Depending on your project and the message you are trying to communicate, you can embellish or distort your letters for effect, as shown in Fig. 9-6 on previous page.

To make your letters or words into an imaginative design, you will need several pieces of layout and graph paper to experiment. On the *Snug-as-a-Bug Coverlet,* the large "S" was first drawn to size, disregarding the squares on the graph paper. Then the rest of the lettering was sketched on the graph for general effect.

After you've developed an overall design, it's necessary to get technical. The letter shapes and curves must be translated into graph units. As a guide for width on the *Snug-as-a-Bug Coverlet,* I counted out the longest line; lowercase letters are 4 spaces wide with 1 space between letters and 3 spaces between words. This makes 25 squares plus 4 spaces for the capital "I" and 7 spaces for the body of the "R" (minus the swash which overlaps the "a"). The total

is 46 squares wide.

After you have a general graph of your project plotted, switch back to creative mode. I changed capital letter sizes, added swashes, and made other additions and alterations. For example, the large "S" fills in the open space in the second row. The swashed leg of the "R" raises the last line of letters closer to the center line to emphasize the rhyme. The upper and lower picket patterns enclose the lettering even more. Experiment with your design until you are satisfied.

About Knitting

The projects in this chapter use two different knitting techniques. The *ABC Knit Coverlet* is plain knitting with a smooth face side and a pebbly back, made by knitting one way and purling (a reversed knit stitch) the return row. The *Snug-as-a-Bug Coverlet* has face knitting on each side—two separate layers of knitting both made at once on the same needles. It's best to become proficient at simple knitting before you try this double technique.

Knitting directions use abbreviations to condense information. Abbreviations used are as follows:

knit (k), purl (p), stitches (sts), repeat (rep), continue (cont), yarn forward toward the knitter for the next stitch (yn.fwd), yarn back away from the knitter (yn.bk). Each project lists the yarn color with abbreviations, too.

Pattern stitches use a combination of knit and purl stitches for different effects. The border is done in a pebble stitch—one knit, one purl repeated with an odd number of stitches. With this the edges curl less than plain knitting, and it does not pull in as does ribbing (one knit, one purl with an even number of stitches).

Lettering appears backwards on the reverse side of knitting. For that reason, and because of all the tied yarns, the *ABC Knit Coverlet* is fabric lined. On the *Snug-as-a-Bug Coverlet* there is no reverse side, but the writing still appears backward on the back. It would be possible, but incredibly complex, to make the wording readable from both sides in the double-knit technique, as you'll see from the directions.

Measuring Gauge

The chart you make may not "make up" the same size it appears. Results vary according to the yarns and needles (or threads and background fabrics for cross-

9-7. The ABC Knit Coverlet *was knitted with a gauge of 4 stitches per inch (2.5cm) by 6 rows per inch (2.5cm).*

stitch). Everyone knits a bit differently, so you need to establish your own gauge by measuring the stitches and rows. To do this, cast on 12 stitches of your yarn, knit 3" (7.5cm), or about 12 rows. If your sample has more stitches per inch (2.5cm) use larger needles. If you have fewer, use smaller needles. Or forget gauge and accept whatever size the coverlet turns out.

For large projects, knitters use 14" (35.5cm) long needles in different sizes to knit flat objects, and turn the knitting at the end of each row, continually knitting to the left. But you can use a circular needle (short needles joined by a stiff wire) and reverse at the end

MATERIALS AND SUPPLIES

Yarn for border and framing. Forest green (G) two 4-ounce skeins knitting worsted, size 4 ply, Orlon acrylic or washable wool.

Yarn for squares and letters. 1 oz. each knitting worsted size 4 ply, Orlon acrylic or washable wool of light yellow (Y), light blue (LB), mint green (MG), pink (P), coral (C), lavender (L), light rust (R), white (W), medium blue (B).

Knitting needles. Size 3 or 4 to suit the gauge of 4 stitches by 6 rows.

Backing. 28" X 36" (76cm X 91.5cm) synthetic jersey knit fabric.

Tools and supplies. Scissors, tape measure, crochet hook size F, 24 yarn bobbins, needle and thread.

ABC KNIT COVERLET

9-8. This knitted coverlet has a knit face and purled back—plus lots of knotted yarns from added colors—so a knit backing fabric was sewn over the center panel in back.

Overview. This crib-size coverlet features block alphabet letters arranged in a 5 X 6 grid. The four extra squares appear within the grid, so at a glance the grid seems to be entirely full of letters. This is a good project for leftover yarns since there are nine colors in small amounts. Only the border and framing color requires more. The coverlet is single knitted with a pebble-stitch edging. A knit-fabric backing is attached by hand sewing. Brief written instructions are given to begin, then follow the chart for the center design.

Technique. Simple knitting and purling are used, even to make the pebble-stitch borders. Changing colors requires bobbins or "butterflies" to hold the yarn colors to keep them from tangling.

Type style. Block, all-cap letters. Each letter fits within a chart 9 stitches wide by 17 rows high, allowing for a fair amount of detail, which is needed to create curved letters like "S" and diagonal ones like "Z." All strokes are two stitches wide or high. The size yarn and needles you use will affect the overall size of the coverlet. See Fig. 9-15 for the complete graph of the alphabet for this project.

Size. 29" X 36" (73.5cm X 91.5cm). Gauge: 4 stitches per inch (2.5cm) X 6 rows per inch (2.5cm). Finished weight is about 18 oz. Thinner yarn and/or smaller needles will create a smaller coverlet.

Color concept. Dark green border and framing with 9 pastel colors for the lettering and blocks.

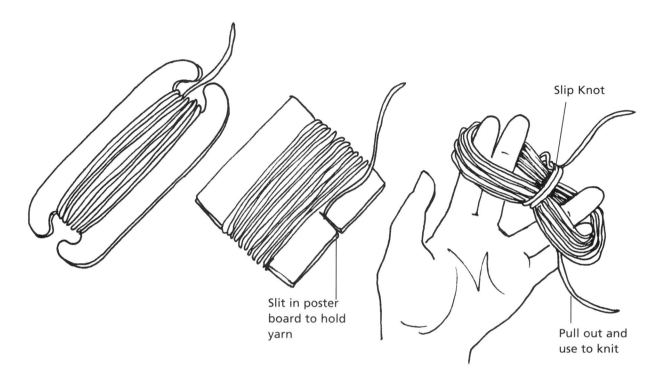

Slip Knot

Slit in poster board to hold yarn

Pull out and use to knit

9-9. There are different ways to keep knitting yarns in order. You can buy commercial shuttles or bobbins (left), or make your own from poster board (center). Another way to keep yarn in order is to wind "butterflies" on your fingers and tie them (right).

of a line. The stitches can't fall off and this eases the weight as the coverlet grows.

Be sure to use washable yarns for baby coverlets. When investing your time in a project, choose quality yarn in colors you really like.

Prepare the Bobbins

Before you start to knit, wind 4 bobbins of forest green and one bobbin of every color—eventually you may need more. Use ready-made bobbins or make your own by cutting cardboard pieces 1" wide (2.5cm) by 3" (7.5cm) long and make a ½" (1.3mm) slit in the 1" (2.5cm) side. Wind the yarn around the long side and pull the knitting end through the slit to keep it from unwinding (see Fig. 9-9).

To work without bobbins, wind "butterflies," as shown in Fig. 9-9. Pull a 3" (7.5cm) tail of yarn

between your middle fingers to start. Hold the hand flat, and wind yarn around your fingers until you have a fat bundle. Clip the end and wrap it around the bundle through your middle fingers. Make a granny knot to hold. Pull yarn out from the tail.

Knit the Coverlet

Work directly from the book and follow the chart as you knit. For the number of stitches, count the squares on the chart for each color. See Fig. 9-10 for the overall pattern, and Fig. 9-15, at the end of this chapter, for the graph of the individual letters. Directions below include general information as a guide. Use an enlarged photocopy if that makes it easier to count stitches as you work. Use a ruler or paper to lay along the row and keep your place.

Instructions are in the caption

for the chart in Fig. 9-16.

1. To pebble stitch the border, cast on 115 sts and knit 1, purl 1 across. Repeat this for 20 rows. The odd number of stitches will offset the knit and purl stitches making the pebble-effect border.

2. To knit the first blocks row, on row 21, knit 1, purl 1 green (G) for 10 sts. Join the first block color of yarn (rust for the "V") by knotting it to G, but don't clip off the G skein. Knit 15 R sts, join a bobbin of G and knit 1, purl 1 for 5 sts. Repeat 15 color sts and 5 G, adding four bobbins Y, W, P, and L, interspersed with three G bobbins. Then add the second G skein for the right border. Keep all the knotted yarn tails on the back side. Your knitting will look like a clothes line strung with bobbins, but imagine trying to keep your yarns untangled without them!

3. On row 22, continue purling

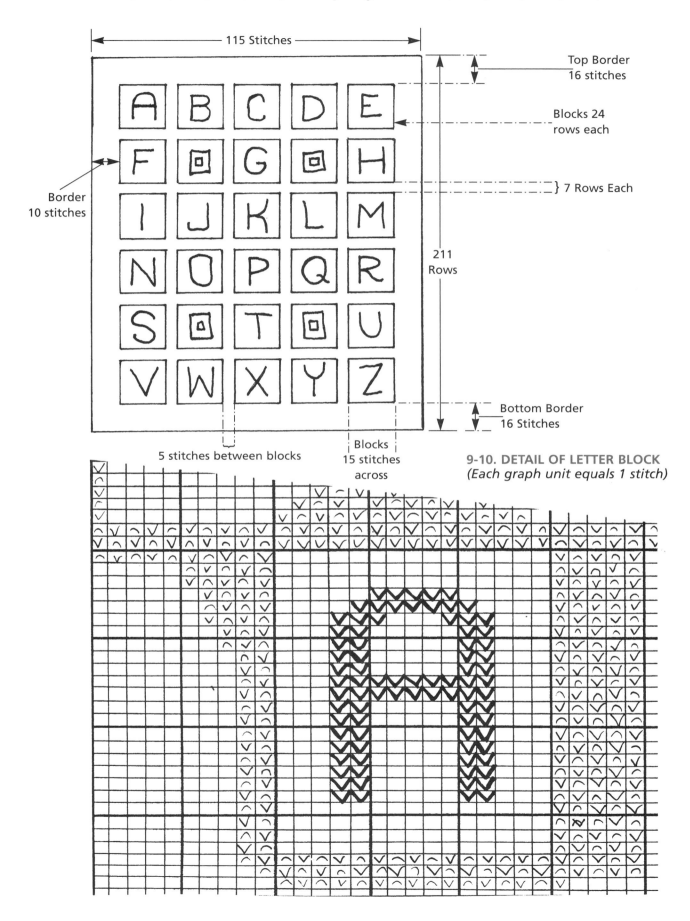

|← 115 Stitches →|

Top Border
16 stitches

Blocks 24
rows each

} 7 Rows Each

211
Rows

Border
10 stitches

Bottom Border
16 Stitches

5 stitches between blocks

Blocks
15 stitches
across

9-10. DETAIL OF LETTER BLOCK
(Each graph unit equals 1 stitch)

each color as you come to it, the same as above. Important: Make sure you twist the yarns to join them whenever you change colors. Holes will appear in the quilt if you don't. Knit four rows in this manner.

4. To knit the letters, in row 25 knit 1, purl 1 for 10 border sts, knit the background color to the letter (7 sts of R for the letter "V") and join the letter color (MG). Knit the letter according to the chart (1 MG st), carry the background color (R) loosely across the back and continue knitting the background color. If there are more than 3 stitches between sections of the letter such as the legs of the "W," join a new bobbin of color to avoid long overshots of carried yarn. Begin letter colors across the entire row.

5. Move up a line on the chart to row 26. Knit 1, purl 1 for 10 border sts, purl across the row, changing colors as you come to them, and knit 1, purl 1 for 10 sts. Twist yarns together when colors meet to join the knitting fabric unless, like the "V," one color knits into another. Continue knitting for the 24 rows needed to make a row of letter blocks. When you come to the end of a color, clip it off, loop it around the next color and knot it to itself, keeping the knot on the back.

6. To knit the sashing row, on row 44, knit 1, purl 1 for 10 border sts, purl across, clipping off each finished block color as you come to it and knot it to itself.

Knit/purl 4 rows and begin the next row of letter blocks.

Continue in this manner until you have finished knitting the entire coverlet.

Finishing the Coverlet

Single crochet all around the edge to stabilize the border. Neaten the knots on the reverse side. To block the coverlet, wash it and arrange it flat to dry. Align the jersey fabric to the quilt back (see Fig. 9-11). Fold hems in the jersey to fit within the border, and hand stitch in place using loose hidden stitches, as shown in Fig. 9-11. Be sure the stitches are stretchy and loose, so the threads will not break when the coverlet is in use.

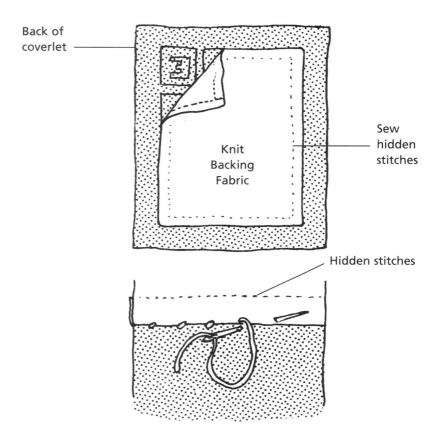

9-11. To complete the coverlet, measure, cut, hem, and sew on knit fabric backing to the coverlet using a hidden, stretchy stitch.

SNUG-AS-A-BUG COVERLET

9-12. The Snug-as-a-Bug Coverlet *is double-sided, which means both sides are knitted at once. The colors are reversed on the back.*

Overview. This baby coverlet features a saying designed into a rectangular central motif. It is knitted double—in two layers with the backside pattern the same as the front (the back is not purled). Colors are reversed on the back as the light front color switches back and forth with the darker back color. If double knitting seems too complicated, you can knit it single thickness using ABC quilt knitting instructions as a guide.

Technique. Double knit, reversing colors.

Type style. Mixed styles are used. Roman capital letters have thick and thin strokes with serifs and swashes (swooping lines added to the serif or stroke for dramatic effect). Block lowercase letters have all the same width strokes.

Size. 33" X 44" (84cm X 111.5cm), including fringes. Gauge: 3 stitches per inch (2.5cm) and 4 rows per inch (2.5cm).

Color concept. Since one color shadows the other, choose two colors that harmonize well, yet have sufficient contrast. A fuzzy washable yarn tends to look best with this double-knit technique, since it blends the colors. The quilt shown is warm white (W) with a variegated mauve, rust and gray-blue yarn (M).

MATERIALS AND SUPPLIES

Yarn. Four 2½ ounce balls white; five 2½ oz. balls mauve. Use a fuzzy, heather-blend, four-ply acrylic yarn.

Knitting Needles. Two size 3 or 4 needles, or an 18" (46cm) circular needle, size 3 or 4. Test the gauge of 3 stitches per inch (2.5cm) as described earlier in this chapter under "Measuring Gauge."

Tools and supplies. Tape measure, scissors, crochet hook (for mistakes), bag or basket for yarns.

Getting Started

To knit this coverlet, read the general directions below, then follow the diagram (see Fig. 9-13) to knit the bottom of the coverlet. When you reach row 46, follow the chart in Fig. 9-16, at the end of this chapter, to knit the central motif. You can work directly from the book, or enlarge the pattern for the central motif on a photocopy machine. Since the borders are not charted, numbers of stitches per row are given in Fig. 9-13 on page 110.

Knit the bottom border first: Cast on 97 mauve sts. For rows 1 to 9; k 1, p 1 all the way across for 97 sts (uneven number), ending in a knit stitch. Turn knitting and repeat back for 9 rows. Begin each row with a knit stitch (which cre-

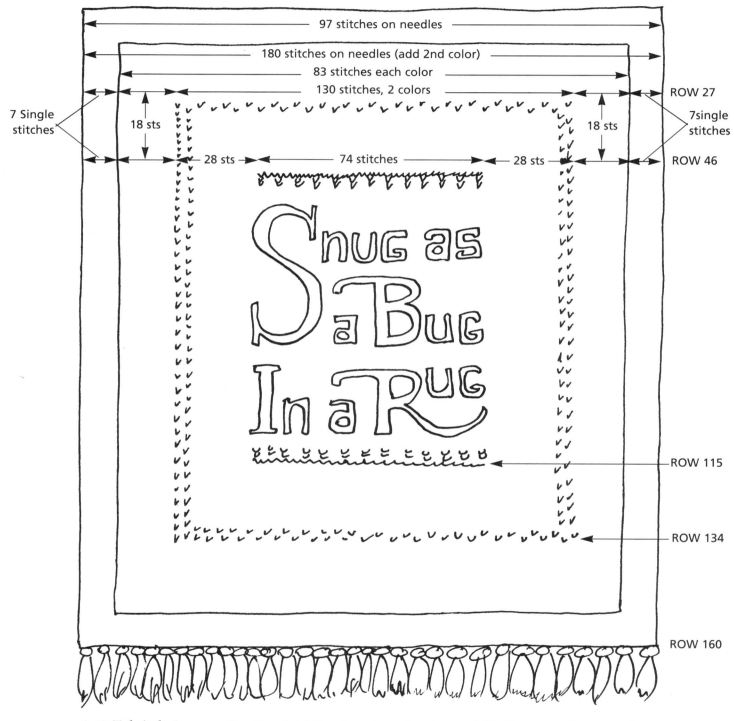

9-13. To knit the Snug-as-a Bug Coverlet *follow the written directions and this diagram until row 46, where the chart begins. Follow the chart, Fig. 9-16, to knit the central pattern.*

ates a purl on the reverse side). The alternating stitches make the pebbles. On row 10 (back side) purl 97 sts across.

Double Knitting

Begin the two-color double knitting on row 11, the face side. Knit the side border stitches; k 1, p 1 for a total of 7 sts. You will now begin doubling the stitches. With both white and mauve yarns on the back side, knit 1 white stitch in the 8th stitch. Pass forward both the mauve and white yarn with the mauve ahead of the white, but do not twist the yarns. Purl 1 mauve stitch also in the 8th stitch.

For the next double-knit stitch, pass both yarns back (white ahead of the mauve), knit 1 white stitch in the 9th stitch, pass both yarns forward (mauve ahead of white—not twisted), and purl 1 mauve stitch also in the 9th stitch. Continue knitting both colors in each stitch across for 83 sts for each color.

It is important to keep the color to be knitted ahead of the other (to the left in right-hand knitting). This keeps them untwisted and "inside" the knitting. Remember that you are knitting two layers of fabric back-to-back. If the yarns are twisted, colors show on the wrong side.

At the end of the row pebble k 1, p 1 the 7 mauve border sts. You will now have 180 sts on the needle; 7 mauve border sts, 83 white k and 83 mauve p sts, and 7 mauve border sts. You will be knitting with these 180 sts on the needle until the border at the opposite end.

Knit the Central Pattern

To begin each successive double row, you must twist the white around the mauve yarn to join the layers. Continue knitting as described, carefully passing the yarns forward and back—untwisted—to form the two separate layers. Only at the border and with pattern stitches do the two layers join. Elsewhere you can actually pull them apart.

To this point, you know you are right when you are knitting white in white and mauve in mauve stitches. At row 26, the central motif begins on the back side. See "Reading the Chart," below, and then continue with the central motif as follows:

1. Begin the pattern on Row 26 as follows: knit the border, k 1 (M), p 1 (M) for 7 sts. Knit the background, k 1 (M), p1 (W) for 18 sts. For the design section, [k 1 (W), p 1 (M), then k 1 (M), p 1 (W) for 6 sts]; repeat this set for 130 sts. Then knit the background, k 1 (M), p 1 (W), for 18 sts, and the border: k 1 (M), p 1 (M) for 7 sts.

2. Row 27, (front side) border, k 1 (M), p 1 (M), for 7 sts. Background, k 1 (W), p 1 (M) for 22 sts. Design section, [k 1 (M), p 1 (W), then k 1 (W), p 1 (M) for 6 sts]; repeat this set for 122 sts.

Then knit the background, k 1 (W), p 1 (M) for 22 sts, and the border, k 1 (M), p 1 (M), for 7 sts.

3. Row 28 (back side) border, k 1 (M), p 1 (M) for 7 sts. Background, k 1 (M), p 1 (W), for 18 sts. Design, k 1 (W), p 1 (M). Center, k 1 (M), p 1 (W) for 126 sts. Design, k 1 (W), p 1 (M). Background, k 1 (M), p 1 (W), for 18 sts. Border, k 1 (M), p 1 (M) for 7 sts.

4. Row 29 border, k 1 (M), p 1 (M), for 7 sts. Background, k 1 (W), p 1 (M) for 22 sts. Design, k 1 (M), p 1 (W). Center, k 1 (W), p 1 (M) for 118 sts. Design, k 1 (W), p 1 (M). Background, k 1 (M), p 1 (W) for 22 sts. Border, k 1 (M), p 1 (M) for 7 sts.

5. Repeat, alternating Rows 28 and 29, until Row 46, then follow the chart in Fig. 9-16 to knit the central motif.

Reading the Chart

On the chart, each unit represents two stitches; one on the front and one on the back (with colors reversed). Only the front side of the coverlet is shown on the chart. This means on even numbered rows (the back side) for each unit you must first knit the reverse of the unit color shown, then purl the unit color shown. On odd rows, first knit the color shown in each unit, then purl the reverse color. Sounds crazy but it works.

As you knit you'll sometimes get two white or two mauve stitches in a row as you switch colors from front to back. Trust the pattern to turn out

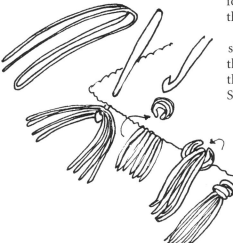

9-14. To make the fringe, cut yarn into sections and double it twice. Insert a crochet hook in edge of the coverlet, pull through a loop of doubled fringe, and pull the tails through the loop.

right, but keep checking with the chart. No doubt you'll make a few blunders and need to take them out if you are new at this—as I was. See "Correcting Mistakes" to correct them. Eventually the rhythm comes naturally and the design will emerge.

Finishing Up

When you arrive at the top border, knit the white and mauve stitches together so you are back to 97 stitches on the needles. Pebble stitch the border.

To add fringes to each end, about one per inch (2.5cm), cut

33 pieces of maroon yarn each 48" (121.5cm) in length. Double it twice to 12" (30.5cm). At the coverlet corner, insert the crochet hook, catch the doubled 12" (30.5cm) fringe in the center and

pull it through. Put both ends through the loop and pull tightly, as shown in Fig. 9-14. Do this every 3 stitches, spacing the fringes across the coverlet. Repeat for the other end.

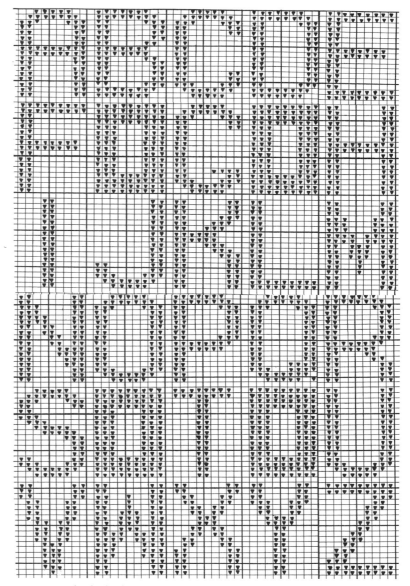

9-15. Graphed Block Alphabet. *Use this "graphed block" alphabet to knit the* ABC *Coverlet.*

9-16 (on facing page). This chart shows the central motif from row 46 to row 115 (numbered up the side). To follow the chart, count units. On the chart each unit represents two stitches; one on the front and one on the back side. On odd rows (front) knit the color given and purl the reverse color. On even rows, knit the reverse color and purl the color given.

CORRECTING MISTAKES

Inspect your work frequently to see if you did it right. Do you have alternating white and mauve stitches? Two kinds of mistakes can occur.

Yarns carried outside across stitches will look like a purl stitch of the wrong color looped over the knit stitch. To repair this, move the knitting on the needles to each side of the mistake. Catch the looped stitch with a crochet hook. Take this stitch off the needle, pull the loop over the stitch on the crochet hook, put the stitch back on the needle and drop the loop in place. If several are wrong, take the row out and redo it.

Twisted stitches will be less apparent, especially with the fuzzy yarn. To repair them you need to take the knitting out back to this point, or hope no one notices it. (There are twisted stitches in my coverlet; fortunately the yarn hides them effectively!)

Each chart unit equals 2 stitches

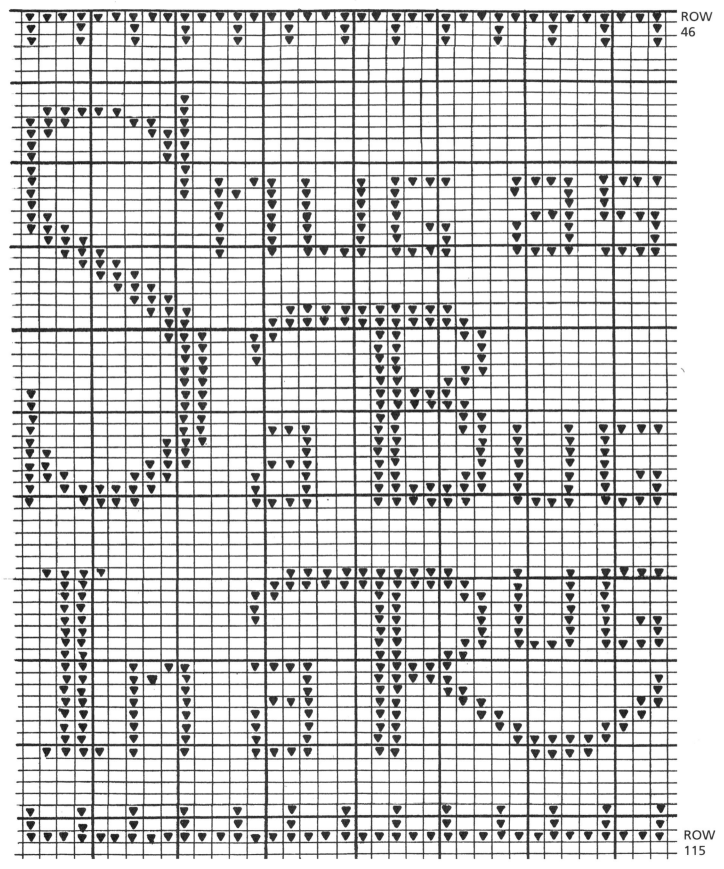

ROW
46

ROW
115

10-1. Letter shapes become so familiar we can recognize them in objects. The ABC Objects Quilt, *which was appliquéd by machine, features letters in the shape of various objects.*

CHAPTER TEN

Designing Type Styles

Letter shapes can be great fun to play with. If you think about it for a minute, you can identify letter shapes everywhere—an A-frame house, an S-curve, a C-clamp, or a V-neck sweater, for example. Letters made in the shapes of objects are not often used for words, but they are used as logos, initial letters, or perhaps to advertise. It's a delightful challenge to make up a typeface using miscellaneous objects or a related series of objects, such as clowns, clothing, cars, cats, colors, or countries.

You'll be surprised to discover what happens to your vision when creating an "objects" alphabet. You begin to see everything in terms of shape rather than utility, need, comfort, or some other focus. Children see faces in

flowers or clowns in the clouds; it's a way of learning their world. Let yourself see as creatively as a child. Give yourself a theme: to make all food shapes, all tools, all sports equipment, all buildings or something beyond imagining.

The above ideas work out best in appliqué, fabric paint, or embroidery, where detail is easy to achieve. A patchwork style alphabet has different requirements. To avoid piecing with tiny bits of fabric, the letters for the *Patchwork Tote Bag* project in this chapter are designed to be cut in larger pieces. If you don't like the way your monogram looks with these letters, you can change them according to the "rules" of this alphabet listed in "Patchwork Alphabet Design Guidelines" on page 116.

Invent an Alphabet

Designers over the centuries have been developing and refining the five basic type styles and pushing them to every limit. A graphics publication called *Upper and Lower Case, the International Journal of Type and Graphic Design* publishes newly invented alphabets monthly, and they are remarkable. All are based on the traditional alphabet shapes, but some are unreadable. Even so they are a lot of fun. Why not try your own invention?

To invent your own alphabet, first develop a concept. Base this on the way you'll construct the letters, on their purpose (whether decorative or utility, for example) on the impression you want to project, the space you need to fill, or a wild idea you have. Say you

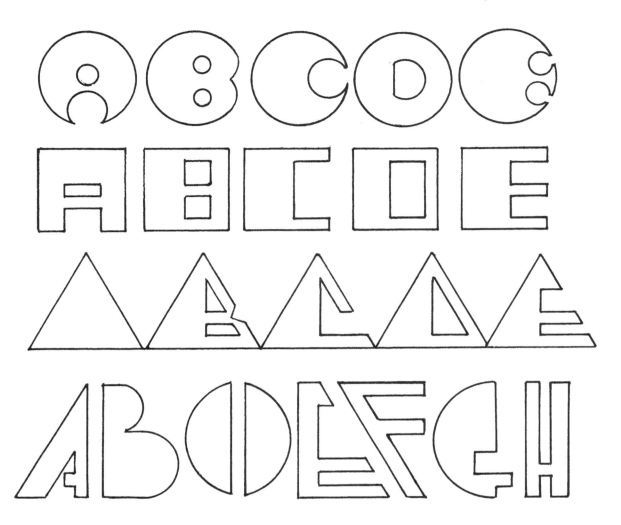

10-2. To invent your own alphabet, start by deciding on an overall concept. These samples show alphabets designed with round, square, triangular and mixed geometric letters.

wanted to make all the letters as round as possible—or square, or triangular. Or maybe you would like the letters to have enough area to contain decorations. Or perhaps you want some incredibly elegant letters. See Fig. 10-2 for some examples to get you started.

If you want to invent your own letters, here are some general guidelines that you will find helpful. They aren't rules, because a clever designer can defy any of them and still succeed.

❖ Make letters similar in size and scale so they don't look like giants and midgets together. (Intriguing image, though, isn't it?)

❖ Make letters of similar visual weight and style, not skinny snakes with hefty houses.

❖ Don't contort the letters so much that they are not recognizable.

❖ Think about construction technique for designing letters to be sewn.

Patchwork Alphabet Design Guide lines

When I designed the alphabet for the *Patchwork Tote Bag*, I gave myself a list of "rules," listed below, to guide the design.

1. Every letter fits in a space 4" (10.25cm) wide by 8" (20.5cm) tall on the tote bag—monogram style—three letters in all.

2. Letters with cross bars divide in the center (not above or below the mid line).

3. Letters assemble by piecing with straight or curved seam lines.

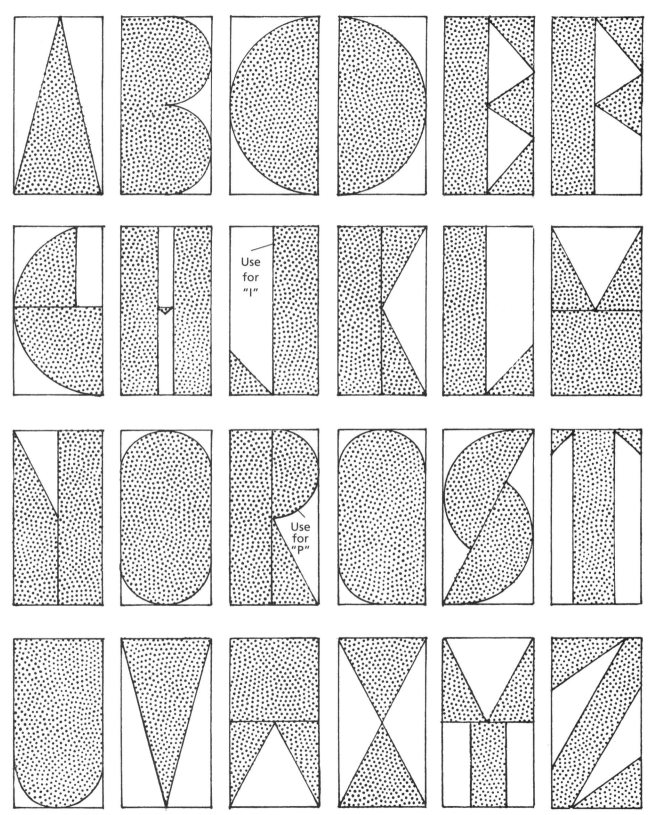

10-3. Patch Alphabet. The letters in this patchwork alphabet were all drawn with straight or curved seam lines made with a ruler or compass. They are designed to be assembled by patchwork and fit into a rectangle.

117

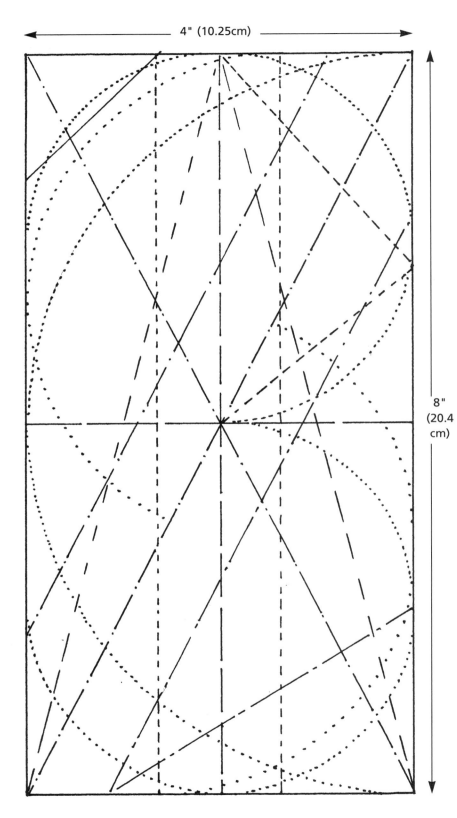

4" (10.25cm)

8"
(20.4
cm)

4. All lines are drawn with a ruler or a compass—with no free-form curves.

5. All letters use about the same area of fabric, so they appear to have similar visual weights.

6. No letters have serifs, swashes, or other furbelows.

To make the pattern or change a given letter, follow the above rules. To experiment with designing other letter shapes for this alphabet, draw yourself a 4" X 8" (10.25cm X 20.5cm) guide like the one in Fig. 10-4. (Or photocopy the one in the book.) Overlay it with tissue paper, follow these general guidelines as you draw, and your letter will "fit" in this alphabet.

10-4. Use this letter guide to make letter patterns on tracing paper. Scale up your monogram letters so each fits within this space. Find the correct lines to make your letters, shifting the tracing paper if necessary. Use a ruler and compass for accuracy, since this becomes your patchwork template.

PATCHWORK TOTE BAG

10-5. The Patchwork Tote Bag *is a handy design that can be made as simple or as complicated as you like. The "CHS" bag, is pieced in solid colors. The "LVG" bag was sewn using solid-color letters set against patches made from a variety of print fabrics.*

Overview. This quilted patchwork tote bag is designed so monogram pieces can be readily cut and seamed with straight or long curved lines.

Technique. This tote bag is made by piecing patches of fabric together. Or you can use the basic tote bag design and apply letters in any way you wish, using appliqué, embroidery, iron-on, paint, or whatever.

Type style. Patchwork letters. See Fig. 10-3 for the entire alphabet.

Size. 14" X 22" (35.5cm X 56cm) plus handles. The overall bag will measure 20" X 28" (53.5cm X 71cm), once it is pieced together and laid flat, before it is sewn together.

Color concept. This is a very flexible pattern that can be made in any colors and prints you like. Two examples are shown: the "CHS" bag features solid colors, and the "LVG" bag uses prints and solids.

MATERIALS AND SUPPLIES

"CHS" bag fabrics. 8" X 28" (20.5cm X 71cm) rust; 8" X 29" (20.5cm X 73.5cm) red; 5" X 28" (12.5cm X 71cm) purple; 5" X 9" (12.5cm X 23cm) gold; 5" X 11" (12.5cm X 28cm) pink; 5" X 10" (12.5cm X 25.5cm) orange.

Black strips, top band, and handles. 29" X 22" (73.5cm X 56cm) black cut into 6 pieces: two top bands 2" X 21" (5cm X 53.5cm); two strips 2" X 29" (5cm X 73.5cm); and two handles 7" X 24" (18cm X 61cm).

Lining. 21" X 29" (53.5cm X 73.5cm) gray.

Recommended fabrics. Choose firmly woven fabrics such as cottons, poly-cottons, denim, or suede cloth. You can also make this bag from leather.

Inner lining. 21"X 29" (53.5cm X 73.5cm) thin bonded batting or a sturdy fabric such as denim.

"LVG" bag fabrics. Each letter will require 5" X 9" (12.5cm X 23cm) blue fabric. Consult the pattern (see Fig. 10-5) for patch sizes, and add ½" (1.3cm) seam allowances all around. Black strips, lining, and inner lining remain the same as for the "CHS" bag.

Tools and supplies. Paper, pencils, a ruler, compass, iron, sewing machine, pins, sharp scissors.

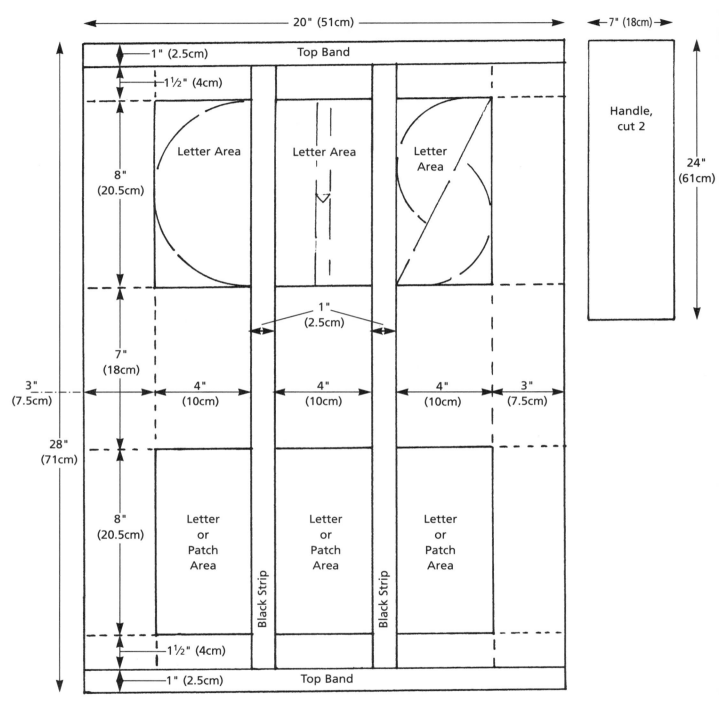

10-6

Make and Cut Out the Pattern

1. To make a letter pattern, draw three spaces on paper that each measure 4" wide by 8" tall (10.25cm X 20.5cm). (Or trace or photocopy Fig. 10-4.) Choose the three letters you plan to use from Fig. 10-3, and scale them up by enlarging them on a photocopier or graphing them to full size. Using a compass, ruler, or other drafting tools, draw each letter to fit into one of the three spaces. (If you are inventing your own letter style, keep in mind how you are going to piece the seams.)

2. Cut the paper pattern apart for template pieces. (You will have pieces both for letters and the pieces that surround them.)

3. Next, select the fabrics you want to use—both for the letters and the rest of the bag. Lay the colors together and see if they sing to your soul. If not, sort through your scraps and choose ones that do.

4. Using your template patterns, trace seam lines around the pieces on the back of the fabrics you selected. Add seam allowances of ½" (1.3cm) on all pieces.

5. Cut out the letter pieces and the pieces of fabric that surround them. Then pin each letter block together.

6. Trace the pieces for the rest of the bag. You can use the pattern (Fig. 10-6) to trace the pieces for the rest of the bag. Add seam allowances (½" [1.3cm]) and cut out these pieces. To cut the fabric for the lining and the back of the bag, you can also measure from the overall dimensions, draw seam lines on the back of the fabric for the bag and lining pieces, and cut them out.

Assemble the Outer Bag

1. First piece the letter blocks. To join straight pieces, pin them together face-to-face through the seam lines. Stitch, open, and press flat. To join curved pieces, such as on "C" and "S," refer to Figs. 10-7 and 10-8. Make short clips on the inside curve to ease the pull of the seam allowances. Fold each curved piece to determine the center, and pin the centers together face-to-face on the seam line. Pin the cor-

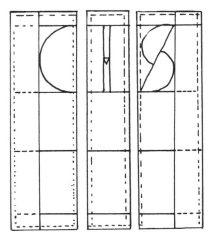

10-9

ners together on the seam lines. Pin through the seam lines inch by inch to align the pieces. The result will look bristly. Machine sew the seam, hand-wheeling over the pins if necessary. Remove the pins and press flat.

2. Piece the bag in sections by first assembling each letter strip, as shown in Fig. 10-9.

3. Join the completed letter strips to the black 2" X 29" (5cm X 73.5cm) strips, aligning horizontal seams (see Fig. 10-10 on page 122).

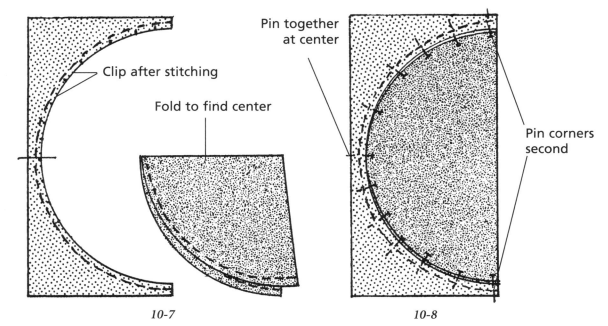

Clip after stitching

Pin together at center

Fold to find center

Pin corners second

10-7

10-8

4. Align the top band, sew, open, and press. Repeat on the other end of the bag.

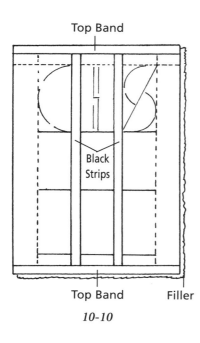

10-10

Assemble the Bag

1. Align the pieced top on the filler or inner lining (see Fig. 10-10) and pin. Machine or hand quilt by sewing "in the ditch" (directly on the seam line) for hidden quilting.

2. To make the handles, refer to Fig. 10-11, and fold the black 7" X 24" (18cm X 61cm) handle fabric lengthwise to 3½" (9cm) wide and press. Fold in the raw edge ½" (1.3cm) and press. Fold in

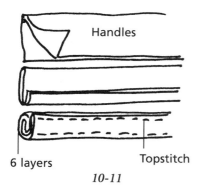

10-11

1" (2.5cm), and fold again so the piece is 1" (2.5cm) wide and 6 layers thick. Press. Topstitch using matching thread the entire length on each side. Repeat for the other handle.

3. To attach the handle, lay one handle on the bag and align each end with the black vertical stripes on the same side of the bag. Leave 2" (5cm) protruding above the top of the bag, as shown in Fig. 10-12. This handle loops, so be sure it is not twisted. Repeat for the other handle.

4. Align the lining face-to-face with the pieced bag—handle ends still sticking out. Sew across the

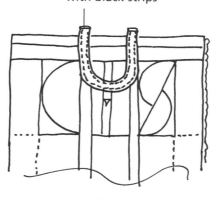

10-12

top edge on each side, stitching the handle ends in place in this seam.

5. Pull the lining and bag apart, align the black strips and top seam line to match exactly on each side.

6. Sew the bag and lining sides closed, leaving an opening in the lining on one side 4" (10cm) long to turn (see Fig. 10-13). Press these seams open. Don't turn yet.

7. From one corner, measure up the side seams for 2½" (6.5cm), fold the corner so the seam is centered, and draw a line across at right angles to the seam. Stitch across the corner and trim

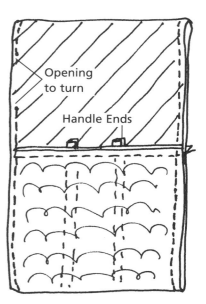

10-13

off the excess (see Fig. 10-14). Repeat for each corner of the bag and lining.

8. Turn the bag right-side-out (see Fig. 10-15). Press the top edge with seam allowances open and smooth inside. Align the handle ends (now inside) flat. Topstitch around the black seam line to secure the lining in place and to reinforce the handles. Sew the opening closed.

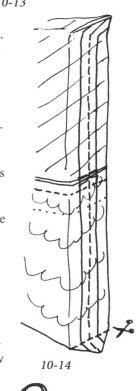

10-14

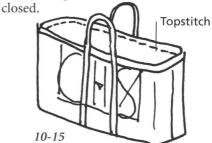

10-15

ABC OBJECTS QUILT

10-16. The ABC Object Quilt *features letters formed in the shapes of various objects. See Fig. 10-1 for a photo of the entire quilt.*

Overview. The letters in this child's quilt or wall hanging are designed as common objects that were selected for their shapes. Letters are appliquéd with a satin-stitch outline, and the shapes outline-quilted.

Technique. Appliqué, quilting, designing, and arranging letters.

Type style. ABC Objects. See Fig. 10-17 for the entire alphabet.

Size. Wall quilt size: 38" X 42" (96.5cm X 106.5cm); center panel is 24" X 28" (61cm X 71cm).

Color concept. All the colors are cheerful and bright and in mid-range hues. This means the yellow is dark enough to show up on white, few really dark colors are used, and colors are mid-range to bright, with few muted hues (taupe and tan, but no cool gray). Colors look cheery, since many of them have a touch of yellow mixed in—including the off-white background. See Color Fig. C-1 for a color photograph of this quilt.

MATERIALS AND SUPPLIES

Center panel fabric. Firmly woven, medium-weight cotton or poly-cotton in warm white or eggshell, 25" X 29" (63.5cm X 73.5cm).

Border fabric. 1 yard medium-weight cotton-mix fabric print (the fabric shown is denim). Cut in four pieces: 2 sides: 8" X 29" (20.5cm X 73.5cm), top and bottom: 39" X 8" (91.5cm X 20.5cm).

Backing fabric. 39" X 43" (99cm X 111.5cm), use the border fabric or a harmonizing color.

Appliqué object letters. Fabric scraps 4" X 6" (10cm X 15cm), more or less, in these colors: egg-yolk yellow (chrome), golden brown, melon, bright pink, orange, red, maroon, medium green, pea green, pin-dot dark green, sky blue (cobalt), blue print, lavender, tan, taupe, black, brown, metallic silver. Use Color Fig. C-1 as a guide or choose your own colors.

Recommended fabric. Firmly woven poly-cotton, cotton, or denim fabrics.

Machine embroidery threads. Bright and a shade darker than colors above for outline or details.

Filler. Bonded poly-fiberfill, 39" X 43" (99cm X 111.5cm).

Tools and supplies. Iron-on stabilizer for objects, long ruler, pencil, tracing paper, iron, sewing machine, sharp scissors, and pins.

Prepare the Pattern and Letters

1. Enlarge the letter pattern (see Fig. 10-17) to size on a photocopier or scale it up on graph paper. (Or, invent your own object letters!)

2. Make a full-sized paper pattern of the center panel for placement (see Fig. 10-19). It can be in more than one piece. You will also use it as stabilizer backing paper. Make two if you want to save one.

3. For the center panel, border, and backing, use a long ruler to measure and draw seam lines on the reverse side of the fabric, adding ½" (1.3cm) seam allowances outside the drawn seam lines.

4. Trace each object letter in reverse on the backing of iron-on fuser (the smooth side). Then iron the fuser (rough side) onto the reverse side of the object letter fabric (see Fig. 10-18). Keep in mind that the cut-out object letter pieces, once they are scaled up, are finished sizes and don't need seam allowances. For two-color objects (the magnet, watermelon, hammer) fuse the whole object in one color; fuse the second color over this. If the bottom color shadows through, fuse these object sections separately.

10-17. ABC Objects Alphabet. This fun alphabet features letters shaped like common, everyday objects.

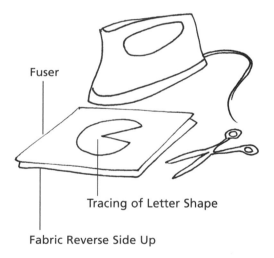

Fuser

Tracing of Letter Shape

Fabric Reverse Side Up

10-18

Appliqué the Objects

1. Pin the full-sized center pattern under the white background fabric. Lay this on the ironing board. On it, arrange the object letters according to the pattern (you can see the pattern through the fabric). Pin or tape the objects in place. Remove the fuser backing and iron each object in place—but don't iron over the pins or tape.

2. Choose machine-embroidery thread colors to affix, outline and highlight the objects. Use colors such as golden yellow for the yellow sun and ocher for the ruler (to differentiate the yellows), red for the orange stand, and melon for the orange snake. Different combinations alter the colors; red with pink looks different from red with green.

3. Baste each letter in place, then satin-stitch over the basting to hold them firmly in place (see Fig. 10-20). Use a medium to wide satin stitch that will overlap into

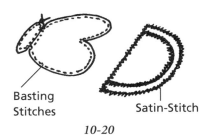

Basting Stitches

Satin-Stitch

10-20

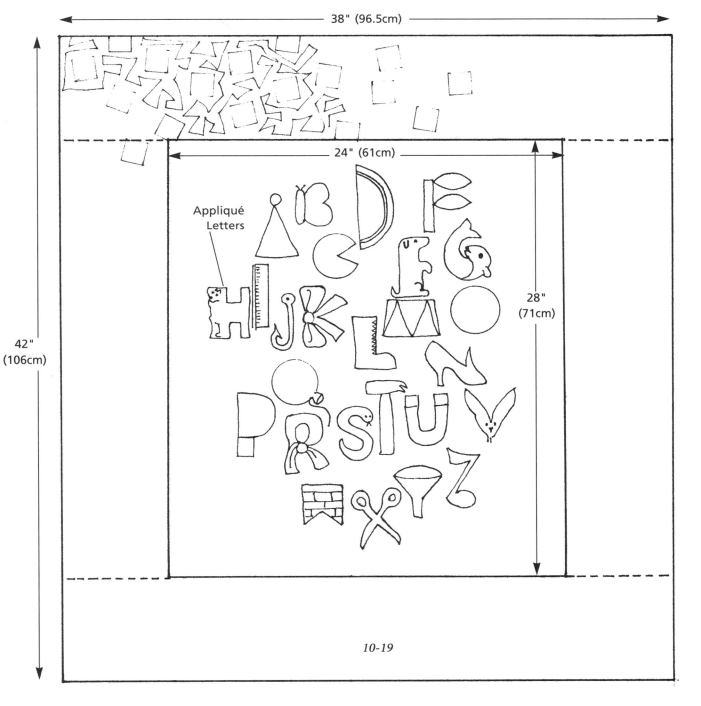

38" (96.5cm)

24" (61cm)

Appliqué Letters

28" (71cm)

42" (106cm)

10-19

the fabric, with the outside edge of the stitch just covering the cut edge.

4. Tear away the paper backing behind the center panel of the quilt.

Assemble the Quilt

NOTE: You may wish to machine quilt the center section first, then add borders as in the quilt-as-you-go technique given for the *Mother Goose Quilt* in Chapter 11, on page 130. Free-motion machine quilting is easier on smaller sections.

1. Align the side border with the center section face-to-face. Pin through the measured and marked pencil seam lines and sew. Open the seam and press the seam away from the light background color. Repeat for the other side border.

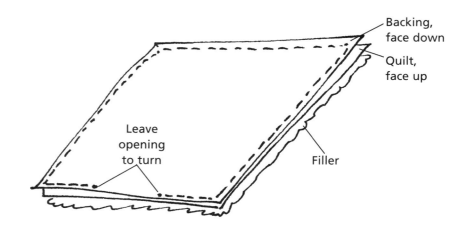

Backing, face down
Quilt, face up
Leave opening to turn
Filler

10-22

10-21

2. Align the bottom border seam lines with the assembled center and side border section face-to-face. Pin on the seam line and sew. Press away from the light fabric, as above. Repeat for the top border (see Fig. 10-21).

3. Lay the cut-to-size filler out flat. Cover it with the completed quilt top, face up. Cover

this with the quilt backing, face down. Align the edges and pin them together on the seam lines.

4. Beginning 12" (30.5cm) from one corner on the bottom, sew through all three layers toward the corner and all around the quilt edge. To sew each corner, angle two short stitches across. Leave a 12" (30.5cm) opening to turn at the bottom (see Fig. 10-22).

5. To anchor the filler before you turn the quilt, machine stitch the filler to the quilt border across the opening, outside the stitch line.

6. Trim away excess filler, grade the seam allowances, and trim across the corners close to the

angled stitching. Turn the quilt. Hand sew the opening closed.

Quilt the Layers

I used free-motion sewing to quilt the *ABC Objects Quilt*, although if you prefer, you can use a large hoop and quilt by hand. Free-motion machine sewing allows you to quilt around the object letters without turning the quilt at every contour, which is easier. However the sewing machine prefers to sew straight forward, so you'll need some muscle to guide the fabric under the needle accurately and keep the layers flat.

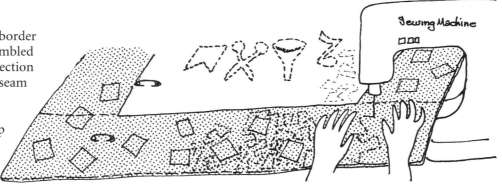

Sewing Machine

10-23

126

To free-motion sew, place your hands like a hoop on either side of the object to be sewn. Guide the fabric under the needle as if you were the feed mechanism. (You are!) Either work slowly and carefully, or full speed ahead and be ready to take out sloppy seams. (In truth, I prefer a combination of these two techniques.) You'll develop a rhythm of fast machine speed and slow movement of fabric. Don't move the fabric during the down cycle of the stitch, or the needle will break and perhaps throw off the machine's timing.

Work on a large flat surface around your machine to support the piece. When you become weary, stop and return later or you'll end up picking out seams.

1. To set up your machine for quilting, use white thread on top and thread that matches the backing in the bobbin. Set your sewing machine to free-motion stitching according to your machine manual. (See Chapter 8 for more on setting your machine for free-motion sewing.

2. Place chrome safety pins through all layers to anchor at 6" 15cm) intervals. Circle an object with $1\frac{1}{2}$" (4cm) quilting pins just before quilting it. Remove pins and do the next object.

3. Quilt around each object. Quilt the borders and the rest of the piece randomly, as shown in Fig. 10-23. Or quilt using your own pattern.

11-1. The Mother Goose Quilt *shows a slightly stuffed (trapuntoed) goose appliquéd on a background of the traditional "Flying Geese" patchwork pattern. Words from an old nursery rhyme are satin-stitched in automatic lettering around the frame.*

CHAPTER ELEVEN

Using Words and Numbers

Sayings, adages, aphorisms, quotes, maxims, and folklore all are encapsulated forms of knowledge that have loads of appeal. You can use these—and numerals, too—to embellish your sewing in a variety of ways. Stitchery on fabric is an age-old way of presenting the words we so enjoy. One of the best-known stitched sayings is "Home Sweet Home." A contemporary version might read "An Attack Cat Lives Here." How styles change. Where once religious quotes were most popular, now sayings come from everywhere, especially television and movies. The "I like it—NOT!" saying from the movie *Wayne's World* is a good example—even people

11-2. Quilt artist Ruth Reynolds uses appliqué and printed letters to convey messages on her comical wall hangings.

who never saw the movie have heard it. It's funny, though, without the movie's special inflection, this sounds like Shakespeare's inverted word order. How beguiling words can be!

Design Guidelines

Illustrations and letters can be combined imaginatively in many ways to design picture books, sports logos, TV commercials, or sign boards, for example. The projects in this chapter illustrate how you can use them in stitchery. You'll find more examples in the color section of this book. The wall-hung *Mother Goose Quilt*, one of the projects for this chapter, tells a story in two age-old ways—with words and pictures.

Once you start looking, you can find pithy sayings everywhere, especially on clothing where the message is often combined with an illustration. Sometimes the style of lettering illustrates the message and sometimes the message is implicit—as with a happy face.

Whatever kind of stitching you do, I encourage you to collect ideas and keep them. Use a sketchbook, clippings file, or a scrapbook—whatever you prefer. Just keep them in a form that makes it easy to tap into them and rework as needed. The *Mother Goose Quilt* was designed for a stuffing company with the goose as an emblem. The idea for it came from my files. I'd put together a photo of the neighbor's pet goose and a nursery rhyme, intending the result to be part of a book. You never know when you may need an idea!

When you plan a project, keep in mind that people prefer text that appears right-side-up and reads from left to right (in English). (Because the story on this quilt is a simple nursery rhyme, it can trail around the border requiring only a little head-twisting to read.) Today, there's a trend toward jamming lettering in willy-nilly for effect. It's up to you to decide how important legibility is to your idea. Some current "cutting edge" graphic work gets so carried away with "design" that you cannot decipher the message. Some calligraphy designs emphasize the type style with little interest in the message. Ask yourself what matters most in your idea.

Color Choices

Color choices affect your message as well. The colors used in the goose quilt are muted or grayed,

MOTHER GOOSE QUILT

Overview. This wall-hung quilt has a trapunto-stuffed appliqué goose over a background made from the traditional Flying Geese quilt pattern. The embroidered lettering was done on a Brother Pacesetter 7000 machine with disk #1. See Color Fig. C-8 for a color photo of this quilt.

Technique. Appliqué with satin stitch outline in trapunto style and piecing. The piece is assembled in quilt-as-you-go sections to allow for appliquéing the center panel by sewing machine.

Type style. Bookman, a roman type style, is similar to the automated typeface used in the project. You can scale up and trace the alphabet given at the end of this chapter (see Fig. 11-23), then machine embroider, hand-sew, photo transfer, or paint these letters.

Size. Overall: 41" X 45" (104cm X 114cm); center goose panel 24" X 28" (61cm X 71cm).

Color concept. The bright white goose with orange feet and bill stands out against the muted colors used to sew the Flying Geese background. The background is sewn in assorted colors as follows: top row: light gray, taupe, light gray-green, light blue, light blue gray. 2nd row: navy with white pin dot, dark blue-gray. 3rd row: gray, maroon, purple. 4th row: bright pink, lavender, purple-pink print. 5th row: black, navy, medium green, gray-green print, gray-blue. 6th row: rust, maroon, orange, taupe with dark pin dot. 7th row: light purple, purple, navy brown, light brown, ecru.

so the bright white and orange of the central figure stand out. One way to get a handsome color scheme is to select a painting or print fabric as a color key. Choose a fabric print that expresses your idea in feeling and key all colors

to it. Even if the fabric is not part of the final design, it can guide your color choices in laying out the design.

On the *Grow Chart*, the other project for this chapter, the color concept is based on the rainbow's

spectrum, but these shimmering colors are difficult to find. Here, instead of primaries, the colors include bright pastels (more pinks than reds) and mixed darker colors (gold instead of yellow, rust instead of red). Instead of repeat-

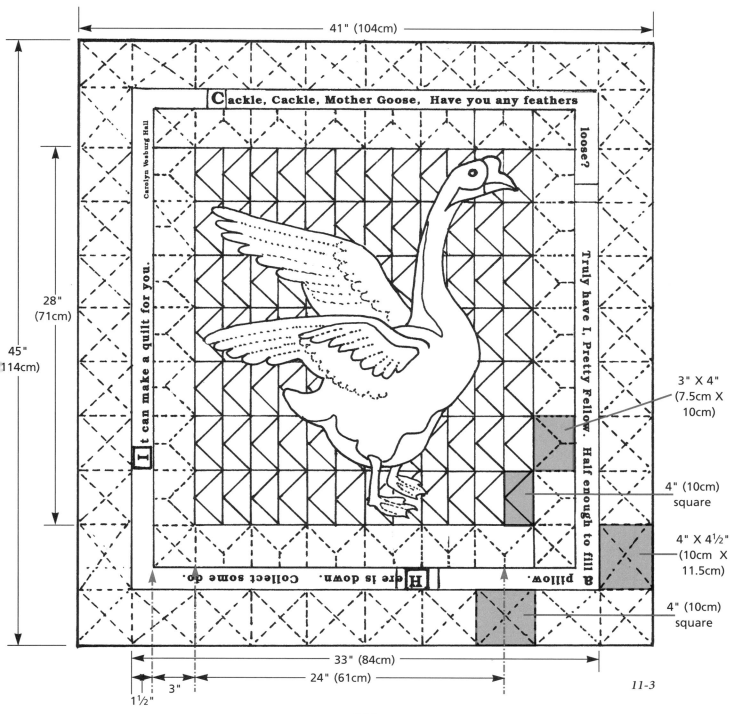

41" (104cm)

28" (71cm)

45" (114cm)

Cackle, Cackle, Mother Goose, Have you any feathers loose?

Carolyn Vosburg Hall

It can make a quilt for you.

Truly have I, Pretty Fellow. Half enough to fill a pillow.

Here is down. Collect some do.

3" X 4" (7.5cm X 10cm)

4" (10cm) square

4" X 4½" (10cm X 11.5cm)

4" (10cm) square

33" (84cm)

24" (61cm)

3"

1½"

11-3

131

MATERIALS AND SUPPLIES

Note: Fabric sizes given include ½" (1.3cm) seam allowances, except as mentioned. Sizes of fabric pieces are approximate. Always use a traced template pattern or measured and marked seam lines for accuracy.

Goose fabric. White 24" X 24" (61cm X 61cm); shading on neck, body, and wings, taupe 12" X 12" (30.5cm X 30.5cm); bill and back foot, orange 4" X 6" (10cm X 15cm); front foot, dark gold, 4" X 6" (10cm X 15cm); eye, black, 1" (2.5cm) sq.

Background fabric. For the Flying Geese pattern you need 84 right triangles 3½" (9cm) each side of the right angle and 4½" (10cm) across the long side. You also need 168 smaller right triangles 2½" X 3¼" (6.5cm X 8.5cm). Note that these measurements include about ¼" (6mm) seam allowance on all sides, the templates in Fig. 11-4 show the actual size of the pieces, without seam allowances.

Frame fabric. Bottom 25" X 4" (63.5cm X 10cm) taupe with dark pin dot; right side 32" X 4" (81.5cm X 10cm) medium blue-gray; top 29" X 4" (73.5cm X 10cm) light gray-blue; left side, 35" X 4" (89cm X 10cm) taupe with dark pin dot.

Lettering strip fabric. Four strips off-white heavy poly-cotton or canvas-weight fabric 4" (10cm) wide (or more) and 40" (101.5cm) long (includes extra). You also need iron-on backing 2" X 40" (5cm X 101.5cm).

Border fabric. Two pieces 41" X 5" (104cm X 12.5cm) and 2 pieces 45" X 5" (111.5cm X 12.5cm), rust with white pin dot.

Backing fabric. Two yards 44" (111.5cm) harmonizing print fabric cut into these sizes: center panel, 25" X 29" (63.5cm X 73.5cm); frame bottom, 25" X 4" (63.5cm X 10cm); frame right, 32" X 4" (81.5cm X 10m); frame top, 28" X 4" (71cm X 10cm); frame left, 35" X 4" (89cm X 10cm); border sides, two pieces 34" X 7" (86.5cm X 18cm); border bottom, 42" X 7" (106.5cm X 18cm); and border top, 49" X 7" (124cm X 18cm).

Recommended fabrics. Use white suede cloth, velveteen, or cotton for the goose; cotton or poly-cotton blend for the quilt.

Filler. Polyester fiberfill bonded stuffing 2 yards 40" X 44" (101.5cm X 111.5cm), cut into the same size and number of pieces as backing.

Threads. Machine embroidery threads in white, orange, taupe, blue-green, dusty pink, copper. Matching sewing threads for quilting.

Tools and supplies. Computer sewing machine (or other ways to apply letters), iron-on fuser, ruler, tracing paper, template paper or plastic, steam iron, sharp scissors.

QUILT-AS-YOU-GO

Both the projects in this chapter use the quilt-as-you-go technique. This method of piecing fabrics together hides raw edges and allows you to assemble a quilt from completed sections. You need not spread out the entire piece. On the *Mother Goose Quilt*, it allowed for satin stitching the appliquéd central motif without having to wrestle the entire quilt through the machine. The *Grow Chart* was made with hidden seams as a way to keep the measurement sections even.

ing the same rainbow in each one-foot section, the colors are varied like the changeable melody of a song.

Make the Patterns

1. Make a full-sized paper pattern of the goose by scaling up the sketch in Fig. 11-3 to size. The center panel is 24" X 28" (61cm X 71cm). You need a goose pattern that is slightly smaller, so it will fit in the panel. You may want to make a duplicate, since this pattern will be destroyed in process.

2. From your scaled-up pattern of the goose, trace patterns on separate pieces of paper for the goose eyes, feet, and bill, as well as the shadings on the goose's neck, body, and wings.

3. Make a template pattern on stiff paper (or plastic) for the background squares, one 4" (10cm) square, and one for each triangle as shown (see Fig. 11-4). Note that seam allowances are added in cutting.

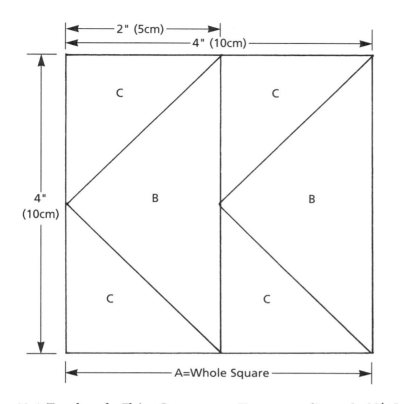

11-4. Templates for Flying Goose pattern. Trace a seam line and add ¼" (6mm) seam allowances. To make the quilt, you will need 84 "B" triangles, and 168 "C" triangles to make 42 whole squares ("A"). (Not to scale.)

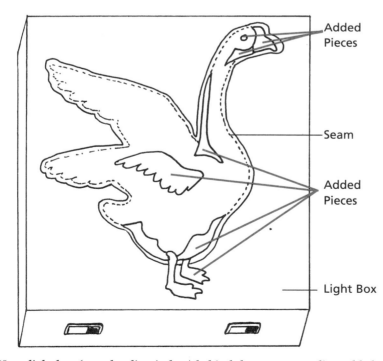

11-5. Use a light box (or a day-lit window) behind the pattern to align added pieces to the goose.

Cut Out the Pattern Pieces

1. First, assemble your fabrics. Either use those listed, or assemble your own. Before cutting and sewing, lay out the entire design to see how colors work together. Change any colors that aren't just right.

2. To trace and cut the pattern pieces, start with the triangles. Trace the template pattern on the back side of the fabric with a pencil. You will use this as a pinning and stitching line later. Add about a ¼" (6mm) seam allowance on all sides when you cut out the pieces.

3. For the larger frame, lettering strip, and border pieces, use a yardstick to draw the seam lines accurately on the reverse side, then add ¼" (6mm) seam allowances when you cut them out. (Don't cut out the lettering strip until after you have applied the lettering.) Use tailor's chalk to draw quilt lines on the face side (or do this later).

4. For the appliquéd goose, trace the pattern on white fabric and cut it out with a 1" (2.5cm) seam allowance. Trace the added pieces (the bill, feet, eye, and shadings on the wings, underbelly, and neck) in reverse onto iron-on fuser paper backing. Iron the fuser on the back of the fabric, cut out the pieces, and iron them in place on the central figure. To align the added pieces use a light box, as shown in Fig. 11-5. Or trace detail lines from the pattern with a removable tracing device, such as disappearing pen, tailor's chalk, basting stitches, or other.

Add the Lettering

The next step is to sew (or otherwise add) the lettering to fabric strips. I did the lettering on this quilt with a Brother Pacesetter 7000 computer sewing machine that has 3 sizes of this typeface. Use a fabric strip wider than necessary in order to get good purchase in the sewing hoop, then cut it to size after sewing. Iron stabilizer backing on the strips. Draw a chalk line or machine baste a straight line as a guide. For more complete information on machine lettering, see Chapter 5.

Each line of lettering starts with an illuminated letter. See "Illuminated Letters" for more on these decorative letters. After sewing the illuminated letters for your quilt, draw seam lines on the reverse side with a pencil 1½" (4cm) apart.

Create the Center Panel

1. First, assemble the patchwork background. To sew the patchwork triangles together, pin them face-to-face through the pencil lines, and stitch on the line (see Fig. 11-8). As you go, press all the seams in the same direction. Six patched triangles make a 4" (10cm) square. Assemble patched squares into horizontal rows—checking dimensions as you go for accuracy. Six 4" (10cm) squares make a row 24" (61cm) wide.

2. Align and stitch the rows together: sew seven rows into a piece 24" X 28" (61cm X 71cm). Continue to press all the seams in the same direction.

3. Next, make a quilt sandwich (see Fig. 11-9). Cut filler and backing fabric each 25" X 29" (63.5cm X 73.5cm). Stack the backing, right side down, under

ILLUMINATED LETTERS

11-6. Illuminate means to light up, or to adorn with brilliant colors. Many Medieval manuscripts were adorned with letters like this one.

Illuminated letters appear-ed originally in beautifully designed hand-drawn manuscripts created in monasteries before the invention of the printing press. These beautiful letters, like the one shown in Fig. 11-6, can be an inspiration for all kinds of stitchery. The *Mother Goose Quilt* gives a nod to this tradition by featuring an illuminated or embellished letter at the beginning of each line. The letters are decorated with added stitching and/or colored fabric patches. To create them on the quilt, sew the patch on first, sew the letter, then add the outline or background trim stitching.

11-7

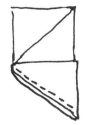

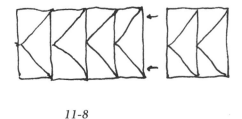

11-8

the filler, and top the sandwich with the patchwork background, right side up. Pin or baste the layers together.

Appliqué the Goose

1. Using machine embroidery thread, appliqué the fused bill, feet, eye, and shadings to the goose. Use a wide satin stitch to cover the edges and to provide decorative lines. Do not sew the goose outline edges yet.

2. Cut out the goose shape in bonded filler. Align goose and filler on the patchwork background, and pin in place. Add more filler if needed. Use a bobbin thread that matches the backing. Machine baste the goose in place, sewing on the line you traced around it. Carefully trim away the seam allowance close to the stitching line. Satin stitch around the goose to outline it as well as quilt the layers (see Fig. 11-9)

3. To sew the detail lines on the goose, pin the paper pattern to the goose, and sew quilting lines for feathers through the paper. Tear away the pattern. Quilt the center panel by stitching "in the ditch," meaning directly on the

seam lines of the patchwork.

Assemble the Frame

The frame is assembled Log-Cabin style. See Fig. 11-10 for diagram of the center panel and all the frame pieces.

1. Align the bottom frame piece to the center panel, face-to-face, and pin through the drawn seam lines. Pin the frame filler on top of the frame piece. On the

Longer backing and filler on all border pieces fold onto back of quilt

11-9

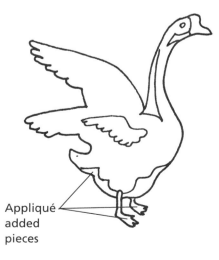

Appliqué added pieces

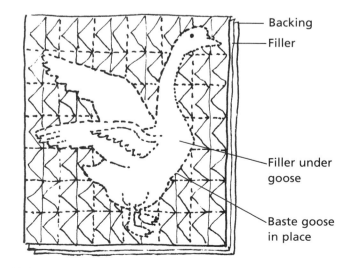

Backing

Filler

Filler under goose

Baste goose in place

11-9

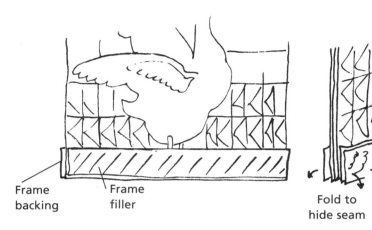

Frame
backing
Frame
filler

Fold to
hide seam

11-11

back, align the backing face-to-face (see Fig. 11-11 on page 136). Then sew through all these layers to attach the bottom frame.

2. Trim away the extra filler, unfold the seam, then press and pin it open. The backing now hides the joining seam.

3. Draw tailor's chalk quilting lines that continue the patchwork quilting lines in the center panel. Stitch them using thread that matches the frame piece on the top and the backing fabric in the bobbin.

4. Align, pin, join, and quilt the right side of the framing in the same manner. Repeat for the top framing and the left side

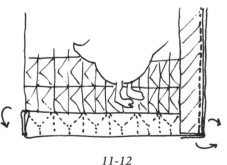

11-12

framing (see Fig. 11-12).

5. To add the lettering strips to the center section, align one strip face-to-face on the border and pin through marked lines. (Double-check to make sure the lettering is oriented in the right direction!) These pieces are extra-long, so you can adjust lettering placement. Sew this seam, open and press. Join the next strips, Log Cabin style, as above. The wider border backing (added next) provides batting and backing for these strips.

Add the Border and Rod Pocket

Note that the borders are assembled and quilted before they are attached to the quilt.

1. To join the border to the filler and backing pieces, stack them with the border backing (cut wider than the top border) face up, the border face down, and the filler on top (see Fig. 11-13). Do this for all

four border sections. Sew the outside edge seam. Press open the seams and fold the backing over to cover the filler and make a finished quilt edge.

2. On the bottom of the border, sew up the side seams to measure 41" (104cm), which is the finished width of the quilt. To make a rod pocket in the top of the border, lay the top border piece flat and hem the sides at 41" (104cm) in width. Hand sew these hems to the filler. Keep this border piece unfolded so you don't quilt the rod pocket shut.

3. On the border pieces, draw tailor's chalk quilting lines that continue the patchwork quilting lines in the center and frame. Stitch them with a border-matching thread on top and a back-matching thread in the bobbin. On the three folded pieces this leaves a 3" (7.5cm) flap of backing and a $1\frac{1}{2}$" (4cm) flap of filler, plus the seam allowance. The top piece is quilted unfolded.

4. Join the border side to the side lettering strip, face-to-face and sew on the marked seam lines through all the layers (see Fig. 11-13). Open and press. On the backing, fold a hem at $1\frac{1}{2}$" (4cm) and hand stitch to the backing (see Fig. 11-14). Or fold and pin a $\frac{1}{4}$"

Finished edge of border

Stitch line
11-14

Wider backing

Border

Wider filler

Stitch line

Unfold
to hide seam

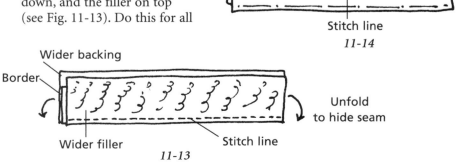

11-13

11-15

(6mm) wider hem, and topstitch in the ditch from the front to secure. Repeat for the other border side.

5. Align the bottom border with the lettering strip, face-to-face, then sew, open, and press. Fold the hem as above and tuck the center and side borders section into the bottom bor-

der. Hand or machine finish as above.

6. Join the top border and center section. Fold the top over at the seam line of border and backing. Fold a hem to align with the lettering seam. Hand or machine sew as above. To finish, hand sew up from the hem 1" (2.5cm) of the rod opening on both sides.

GROW CHART

Overview. This colorful fabric wall hanging will keep a growth record of your children and grandchildren—and would make a great present for any new parent. Notations about each child's height can be sewn on, written in permanent ink, or simply pinned in place. If you are a tall family, add another foot to the design. NOTE: Although metric measurements are included for making this chart, you will need to redesign it for measuring a child metrically.

Technique. The wall hanging is made by piecing strips of fabric onto a backing with hidden seams. The large numbers are appliquéd, the smaller numbers for each measurement were machine embroidered. (I used a Viking 300 sewing machine.) You can make the entire piece by iron-on adhesive appliqué if you wish. Do not stuff this wall hanging, since stuffing will shorten the distance between inch marks.

Type style. "Carousel" numerals are wide enough for appliqué yet rhythmic and playful with the round-ball serifs.

Color concept. I used muted or bright pastel colors in the rainbow spectrum. You can choose instead high-intensity primary and secondary colors arranged chromatically within each foot section: lavender, purple, blue, blue-green, green, chartreuse, yellow, yellow orange, red-orange, red, and rosy fuchsia. **Size.** 65½" tall by 12" wide (158cm X 33cm).

11-16. This Grow Chart *is ideal for keeping a record of how quickly your children or grandchildren grow. It would also make an ideal baby gift. It's shown here with Bradley Stroud measuring himself.*

MATERIALS AND SUPPLIES

NOTE: Measurements include ½" (1.3cm) seam allowances.

Colored strips. 55 assorted strips, 13" X 2" (33cm X 5cm) in assorted rainbow colors ranging from lavender to fuchsia, or bright primaries.

Black strips. Five 13" X 2" (33cm X 5cm); two edge pieces, 2" X 61" (5cm X 154.5cm).

Inner backing. 67" X 13" (170cm X 33cm) heavyweight firmly woven fabric.

Backing fabric. 67" X 13" (170cm X 33cm) denim.

Large numeral fabric. Five pieces 7" X 9" (18cm X 23cm) opaque white cotton fabric.

Triangle top. 13" X 6½" (33 X 16.5cm) print. I used a navy and gold print.

Recommended fabrics. Poly-cotton percale or cotton for front of chart; denim or broadcloth for backing. Use a firmly woven fabric.

Threads. Machine embroidery thread in white and black, gray sewing thread.

Tools and supplies. Scissors, rotary cutter (or paper cutter), a grid-marked cutting mat if you have one, metal ruler, #2 pencil, masking tape, iron, iron-on fusible.

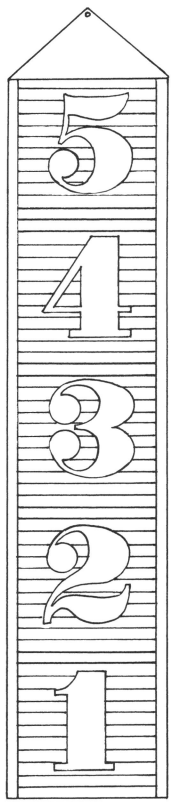

11-17

Getting Started

Instead of making a separate pattern for the *Grow Chart*, the seam lines for the strips are drawn in pencil on the back of the backing strip, which then becomes the pattern. You will use the pencil lines as a guide to sew on the strips. Keep a ruler handy and check measurements as you go. Since the strips on this project measure inches, accuracy is important.

1. First, mark the seam lines on the back of the backing strip. To do this, tape the inner backing strip securely face down on a hard surface. A cutting mat with a grid is ideal to keep it aligned accurately so the fabric does not shift. Draw the seam lines with a sharp pencil using a metal ruler or wooden yardstick. Pull the pencil along so the point doesn't catch on the fabric. Draw seam lines ½" (1.3cm) in from the edges around the strip. Draw a pencil line across the strip every inch for 60 inches. Draw vertical lines for sewn numbers in 1½" (4cm) from the left side (right side on the front). Draw a peak at the top 5½" (14cm) high. Be sure to keep inch lines accurate horizontally. Use a T-square, a right-angle triangle, or the grid markings on the cutting mat.

2. Still working on the back of the backing fabric, number each row from 1 to 60 with a pencil, starting at the bottom. These numerals will help you keep the strips straight as you sew.

3. Cut out the rest of the pieces, including the black strips, the colored strips, and the triangle top, using the measurements listed above. Use Color Fig. C-4 as a guide for cutting out the colored strips, or design your own pattern. If you would like to have a specific color arrangement, number each strip in pencil on the back of the

138

fabric from 1 to 60—corresponding to the numbers on the back of the backing fabric. Keep in mind that every twelfth strip is black.

Assemble the Strips

1. Turn the inner backing face up. Beginning at the bottom, align the first color strip (I used purple) face up on the face side of the inner backing. Line it up with the bottom edge, so it extends up over the seam line you drew on the back. Align the second strip on the first, face-to-face, so it, too, covers the seam line by ½" (1.3cm), as shown in Fig. 11-18). Pin outside of any seam lines.

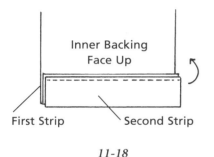

11-18

2. Turn the piece over so you can see the pencil lines again. Then sew across the first pencil line, including the two strips in the seam line. Remove any pins. Trim seam allowances to ⅜" (1cm), grading the one underneath shorter than the one on top. Fold up the second strip and press the seam open. This conceals the seam. The second strip now overlaps the second pencil line (the number-two inch mark) by ½".

3. Align the third strip on the second, face-to-face (see Fig. 11-19). Pin and sew across. Then trim, flip up the strip, and press. As you work, be sure to keep the backing flat so the strips do not pull in, which would shorten the inch marks. Check measurements

as you add strips. (If keeping inch marks accurate is too difficult, you can make the wall hanging in one-foot sections and piece them together.)

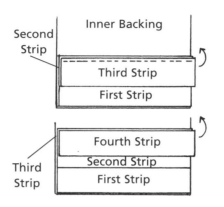

11-19

4. Repeat step 1 through 3 for each added strip. Make each foot mark strip (seam lines 12, 24, 36, 48, 60) black. This gives an orderly stained-glass-window effect. Roll and pin the piece as you sew to make the length easier to handle. NOTE: If a light-colored strip shadows—shows the seam allowance through—line it with white fabric before seaming in place.

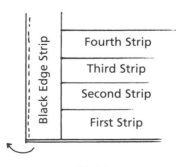

11-20

5. To add the trim pieces, align the vertical black edge strips face-to-face over the marked seam lines and pin in place (see Fig. 11-20). Sew from the reverse side. Flip

11-21

open the black strips and press. Trim the edges even.

6. To add the triangular peak, align the peak fabric over the top strip, face-to-face, and sew (see Fig. 11-21). Flip up and press.

Apply the Numerals

You may want to review the information on appliqué in Chapter 3 and 6 and on automatic machine embroidery in Chapter 5.

1. Scale up or enlarge the numerals to 8" (20.5cm) high. Trace the large numerals in reverse on iron-on fusible paper. Align the numeral with the white fabric grain and iron onto the reverse side. NOTE: If this fabric fails to hide the stripes underneath, use a double layer of white fabric fused together.

2. Peel off the paper backing. The numeral may now distort so place it accurately, as shown on the pattern, and iron it in place (see Fig. 11-21).

3. Pin tear-away backing or paper stabilizer to the lining under the numerals. Using the machine-embroidery thread, satin-stitch around each numeral to cover the edge and hold it in place. Tear off the backing. Here is

a tip for satin-stitching: Sew around the numbers clockwise so you can watch the right edge and maneuver the fabric on the left. Set the stitch to 4.5mm wide, and sew so the outer edge just covers the raw edge. Ease the presser foot a notch if you can, so the fabric moves easier on the curves. Roll and secure the chart so it won't catch on the machine and misalign your stitching.

4. Using black thread, machine embroider the "inch" numerals along the right edge. Be sure to

keep them in an even vertical row.

5. To finish the piece, align the denim backing and the finished front, face-to-face, and pin (see Fig. 11-22). Sew around the entire piece on the seam line, leaving the bottom open to turn. Turn and press. Topstitch in-the-ditch along the black border. Machine or hand-sew the bottom closed.

To hang, put a grommet in the top, or sew a loop. When you hang the *Grow Chart*, be sure to hang it so the measurements are accurate.

Front face up

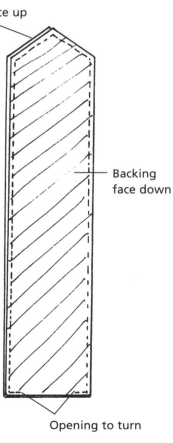

Backing face down

Opening to turn

11-22

ABCDEFG HIJKLMN OPQRSTU VWXYZ & abcdefghi jklmnopq rstuvwxyz

11-23. Bookman Alphabet. This roman type style often is similar to the automated Brother type face used in the Mother Goose Quilt. *You can scale up and trace the alphabet given, then machine embroider, hand-sew, phototransfer, or paint these letters on.*

CHAPTER TWELVE

Three-Dimensional Lettering

Up to this point, the alphabet stichery we have explored has been, for the most part, two dimensional. Although embroidery has a slight three-dimensional effect, the projects in this chapter explore the third dimension a bit more fully. The first project uses trapunto lettering on a bas-relief boot. Trapunto creates lettering raised in low relief, and uses light and shadow to create dimension, not unlike the words and faces on coins or Greek temple friezes. The letters are done graffiti-style, a writing style that one or another rascal has used to leave messages in public for millenniums. Paint-can graffiti on European walls and U.S. subway cars is a prime example, see Fig. 12-4 for the entire alphabet.

The second project details how to make fully three-dimensional letters, which can be used as decorations for a child's room, gifts, or pillows.

Design Considerations

Making sculpture in fabric is most similar to making covers for bodies (clothing) or furniture. Stuffed fabric shapes always tend to roundness like balloons blowing up; upholstered shapes, less so. Sew a square pillow, stuff it full, and it will plump up in the middle, curve in at the sides, and poke out at the corners. The same thing happens with block letters having sharp corners. For this reason, the *Three-D ABC Letters* are "boxed" on the edges with an edging strip of consistent thickness, which helps prevent this. Boxing the let-

ters also helped eliminate problems with pulling or closely trimmed seam allowances on inside corners.

The way a piece is constructed influences shape. Skinny letters when stuffed will flop limply or look like wrinkled hot dogs. Making the letter strokes wider diminishes this and allows for easier stuffing. That's why I used a type style called Tuba, which has extra-thick strokes, to create the *Three-D ABC Letters*.

The kind of stuffing also affects shape. Pieces to be stuffed must be wide enough to stuff, and shaped so you can get stuffing into them. (This tended to eliminate letters sewn with holes in them; I used buttons to represent holes instead.) The letter shapes also suggested a firm stuffing such as polyurethane foam cut to shape, like upholstery, although the letters can also be stuffed with loose foam.

Taking all of the above into account, I arrived at the mechanical roundness of the letters made with a circle guide and right triangle. They aren't perfect. One-legged letters like "P" or "T," may not stand up alone, especially if they aren't symmetrical, and bottom-curved letters, like "O," will roll. But the shapes in the Tuba alphabet are fun (see Fig. 12-17 at the end of this chapter).

If you want to design a different type style, consider making your soft sculpture alphabet with wide square bottoms to remain upright, or with shifting stuffing for a lazy look, or small to wear as jewelry, or large to use as autograph pillows.

Fabrics

Many different fabrics will do for trapunto or soft sculpture. Just think of pillows and the great variety or textures, weaves and weights you've seen. Relate the fabrics to the use. For pillows consider velveteen, corduroy, suede cloth, or washable wool. Light reflects off these dimensional fabrics beautifully. For toys use poly-cottons, denim, synthetics, flannel. For decorations or jewelry use metallics, satins, and ribbon trims. For autograph pillows keep the fabric smooth and plain so they can be inscribed. Use fabrics with some "give" for trapunto so they will mound softly.

Don't forget how fabrics feel. Children often choose something textured and soft for a beloved object—a fuzzy bear or silky blanket, for example. Okay, so maybe yours prefer a metal truck or plastic alien. These, too, have a distinctive touch, even if they are harder to sleep on.

Choose a firmly woven fabric

12-1. The name on the Cowboy Boot Christmas Stocking *was sewn using trapunto, which gives a three-dimensional character to the lettering. The boot is a gift for artist Glenn Elvig, a Minnesota woodworker, who likes boots.*

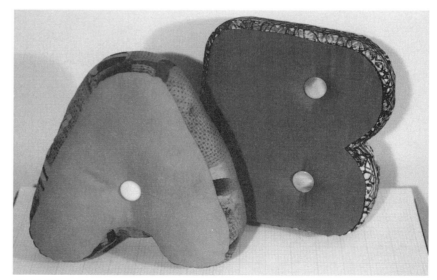

12-2. The soft sculpture letter "A" is made with a boxed edge and softly stuffed for a cushiony appearance. The "B" fits over a foam shape cut out with an electric kitchen knife.

to make the letters that won't fray at the inside corners when sewn, trimmed, and stuffed. Add seam allowance width according to the fabric's potential to ravel or pull out: ¼" (6cm) for poly-cotton, ½" (1.3cm) for wool or velveteen. You can use scrap fabrics pieced together. Seam them together at inside corners to strengthen them or piece them where you will.

Colors

Coordinate the colors. "A" has a bright pink face and a batik edge fabric in bright pink, purple, and orange. In buying new for an alphabet of letters, select a group of fabrics that all go with each other and then mix and match at will for the entire alphabet.

If you are working from your scrap pile, sort out a heap of similar fabrics that relate in color (no matter how wild) and pick letter combinations. Is "A" antic? "B" beautiful? "C" colorful? "D" dark? "E" elegant? "F" fuzzy? "G" gaudy? Use any color concept you like, depending on how the letters will be used.

Just out of curiosity, what colors did you pick? Pastels because children are sweet things? Jungle prints because they are wild? Coordinated colors so children will learn the value of control and color relationships? Did you use every color and texture of fabric you've got on hand so children will learn that life is full of variety and contradiction?

I'm extraordinarily picky about colors and will go to great lengths to get the "right" ones together. As an artist I love the power of color. For fabric users color and texture are the primary components, so use them with power.

COWBOY BOOT CHRISTMAS STOCKING

Overview. This boot is made from small amounts of various colored felt and decorated with embroidery, cut-work, faux jewels, and metal beads. You can customize this project by creating a shoe or boot that suits the recipient. See Fig. 12-3 for some ideas. Then add fringed trim, sequins, fake lizard or other decorations as you see fit.

12-3. Make the boot in different colors or other shapes to suit the occasion and recipient. Try making a fireman's book, ballet shoe, an ice skate, and a traditional stocking, to name a few.

Technique. Several techniques are used in this project: trapunto lettering, cut-work embroidery, free-motion embroidery, topstitching, patterned machine embroidery, and glued-on embellishments.

Type style. Graffiti. In this style, the letters are formed with a big swinging outline stroke overlap, so words appear joined as unit. Usually all letters are drawn the same height in block capitals, but you can do lowercase letters this way, too.

Size. 11" X 15" (28cm X 38cm).

Make the Pattern and Cut Out the Pieces

1. Scale up the pattern to size (see Figs. 12-18 and 12-19 at the end of this chapter). Use the Graffiti alphabet, Fig 12-4, to trace a pattern for the name you want, or use any other fat letter style. If the name is too long, make the letters smaller, or angle the name across the boot and re-design the decorative stitching and trim.

2. Trace the pattern on tracing paper.

3. Pin the pattern on the top piece of tan felt. Poke the pencil tip through the pattern where marked to indicate cut-work sections.

4. Cut out all the pieces according to the pattern. Cut four tan boot tops (two are lining), two boot feet, two boot heels, two boot tabs, two boot edgings and one underlay fabric.

5. Cut out the leaf cut-work designs. To do this fold the felt from tip to tip of each leaf and cut along the dots (see Fig. 12-5). Be sure no pencil mark remains.

6. Re-pin the tracing paper pattern to the boot top.

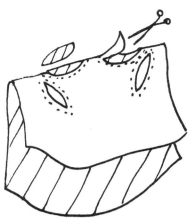

12-5

MATERIALS AND SUPPLIES

Felt for boot. Boot top, four pieces 8" X 11 (20.5cm X 28cm) tan felt; top edging, two pieces 1½" X 11" (4cm X 28cm) white felt; pull tabs, two pieces 1" X 4" (2.5cm X 10cm) rust brown felt; boot foot, two irregular pieces 7 X 11 (18cm X 28cm) rust brown felt; heel, two pieces 3" X 3" (7.5cm X 7.5cm) brown felt.

Inset for cut work. 3" X 5" (7.5cm X 12.5cm) fuchsia metallic fabric.

Tools and supplies. A small amount of poly-fiberfill for letters and heel, machine embroidery thread in maroon and white, six faux jewels in red, six silver beads, sharp scissors, tracing paper for pattern, pencil, sewing machine (Viking/Husqvarna 1200-300).

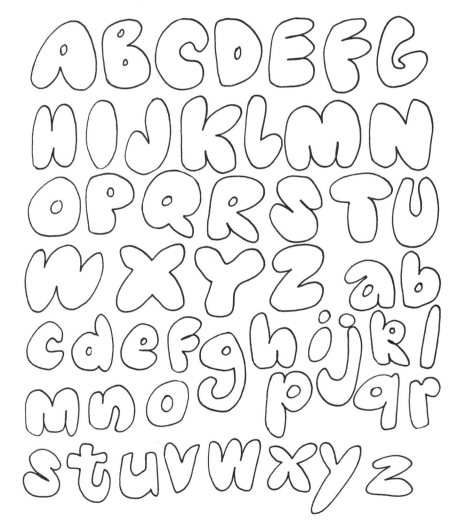

12-4. Graffitti Alphabet. Letters like the ones in this alphabet are ideal for trapunto stitching. To make these letters, begin the stroke at the bottom and swing around the letter with a free-flowing movement to outline its shape all in one continuous line. Graffiti painters shade letters with a can of spray paint; trapunto letters are shaded by shadows.

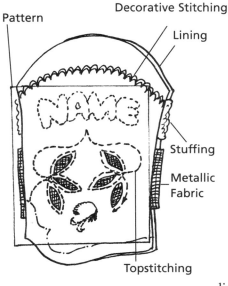

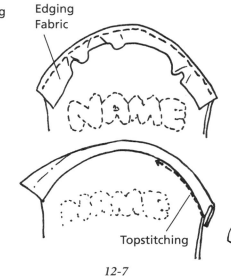

12-6

12-7

12-8

12-9

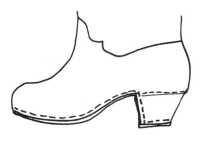

12-10

Decorate the Boot

1. Align the boot top with the boot top lining. Align the inset metallic fabric under the cut-out leaves (see Fig. 12-6). Pin, outside the stitching lines, through all three layers and the tracing paper. Using maroon thread, topstitch (free-motion if you wish) on the leaf outlines. If the pattern outlines do not line up with the cut-out leaves, follow the contour of the leaves.

2. Put a ½" (1.3cm) layer of fiberfill under the lettering (see Fig. 12-6). Using maroon thread, outline the letters. Unpin, open the layers and clip off stuffing that extends beyond the letters. NOTE: If the letters do not appear puffy enough, make slits in the backing and push in additional fiberfill with the scissors point or a knitting needle. Hand sew these slashes closed. (In this case, you may wish to add another lining to this piece, as I did; it's neater).

3. Change to white embroidery thread and sew the topstitching. Tear off all the paper pattern. Set the sewing machine to decorative patterns like those shown and sew the emblem and the scalloped line across the top.

4. Align the white edging strip on the boot top and sew a ¼" (6mm) seam along the top edge. Open this seam and press the edging upward. Fold the edging over the seam allowance and press in place. Pin and topstitch this edging in place (see Fig. 12-7). Trim away the extra.

5. Align the boot foot (rust) with the boot top. Repeat for the boot back. On the front, topstitch a double row along the joining. Machine embroider the decorative lines. On the back of the boot you can embroider your name and the year you gave this gift.

6. Topstitch the pull tabs. Align them on the top of the boot. Sew across the base of the tab so both ends of the tab are included in this seam. Repeat for the boot back.

7. Align the edges to join the boot heel to the boot foot. Open the seam and press. Topstitch the seam. Repeat for the boot back (see Fig. 12-8).

Assemble the Boot

1. Lay the completed boot front and back together, face-to-face (see Fig. 12-9). Stitch the front seam from top to toe. Sew the back seam from tip to heel tip.

Reinforce the stitching over the top edging and trim the seam allowances close to the stitching. Turn the boot and press carefully.

2. Topstitch across the boot sole, turning at the heel to topstitch the heel (see Fig. 12-10). Trim the seam allowances evenly across.

3. Using fabric/plastic glue, glue the jewels and beads in place.

145

MATERIALS AND SUPPLIES

Front and back of letter. Each letter (except "I") takes about 9" X 18" (23cm X 46cm). Use a tightly woven fabric.

Edge (side) of letter. Each letter takes about a 36" (91.5cm) strip of fabric, 3" to 4" (7.5cm to 10cm). The narrower "I" takes 21" (53.5cm). Use a tightly woven fabric. NOTE: To determine the edge length, use a tape measure to measure the outline of your pattern. With 8" (20.5) high letters, the letter "A" takes a strip about 30" (76cm), "M" takes 34," and "K" takes 34. Add 1"(2.5cm) for end seam allowances and another because—as the old saying goes—you can't cut fabric longer if it's too short. For strip side-seam allowances add ¼" (6mm) or the same amount as added for the letter, depending on fabric type.

Trim. Buttons for letter centers as needed.

Filler. Bag of fiberfill loose stuffing or urethane foam 2 to 3" (5cm to 7.5cm) thick cut to shape.

Tools and supplies. Sharp scissors, sewing machine, threads, tape measure, paper for pattern, drafting tools (ruler, T-square, circle guides), pencils, electric knife, and a long needle such as a doll needle.

THREE-D ABC LETTERS

12-11. You meet nearly all the pleasures and problems of making soft sculpture in the construction of the Three-D ABC Letters, including sewing seams for shape and stuffing them for appearance.

Overview. These three-dimensional alphabet letters can be made in different sizes and used as children's toys, pillows, or gifts. Make the ABCs or sew a child's name.

Technique. Soft sculpture.

Type style. Tuba letters have wide strokes that make them suitable for soft sculpture. See Fig. 12-17 at the end of the chapter for the entire alphabet.

Size. All letters are 8" (20.5cm) high. They vary from 3" (7.5cm) to 8" (20.5cm) in width and are 2" to 3" (5cm to 7.5cm) thick, depending on the filler in them. For pillows, if you wish, double the size to 16" (40.5cm), but not the thickness.

Color concept. Use cheerful colors. Each letter has three pieces—the face, the edges, and the back—allowing for two or more fabrics per piece. For autograph pillows or a children's alphabet letters, keep the face fabric plain so the letter is more recognizable. Use print fabrics for fun on the edges, and for the back to tell that the letter is reversed.

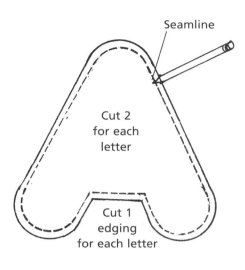

Seamline

Cut 2
for each
letter

Cut 1
edging
for each letter

12-12

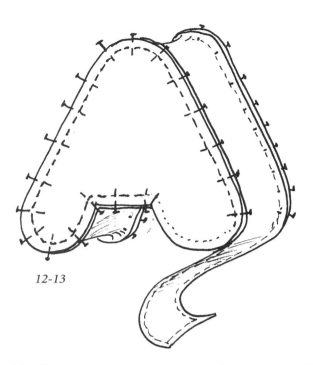

12-13

Make Templates and Cut Out the Pieces

To make templates, scale up the letters you want to sew to size—8" (20.5cm) high, from Fig. 12-17, the Tuba Alphabet. Use tracing paper, newsprint, or copy paper, or photocopy them to size. Use drafting tools to make letters accurate. Trace the letter outline on the back of the fabric to use as a seam line. (You can simply add a ¼" [6mm] seam allowance and sew, but for accuracy, I prefer using a traced template, since my seam allowances can get pretty casual when I'm trying to fit patterns onto fabric scraps.)

Cut out the pattern pieces in the fabrics you have selected. You need a front and a back for each letter, plus an edging piece. Cut the edging piece longer than you need it. Be sure to add a seam allowance on all sides of all pieces, letting the fabric's potential to ravel or pull out determine the width (see Fig. 12-12). For firmly-woven poly-cotton, ¼" (6mm) is fine. Use ½" (1.3cm) for wool or velveteen. If you use satin or similar fabric, use iron-on adhesive lining to prevent fraying and pulling out at the corners.

Assemble the Letters

1. Align and pin the seam lines. Using the "A" as an example, insert a pin in the seam line at one corner of the edge piece (see Fig. 12-13). Align this pin with the inside corner seam line of the "A." Pin through the seam lines matching them every ½" (1.3cm) or less especially around the curves. Make the edge fabric on the corners fractionally longer than the "A" seam line for a better look when turned and stuffed. Leave pin heads sticking outside the fabric. Use an extra-long edging piece to be sure ends meet. If the edge is short, seam on another piece.

2. Sew the seams. Use a short machine stitch exactly on the seam line. Remove pins just as you come to them (and before you sew on them). Pivot on the second inside corner making a short stitch across to accommodate the clipped seam allowance (see Fig. 12-14). Match the edge ends and seam across. Repeat Steps 3 and 4 to join the "A" back to the edge, except leave a 3" (7.5cm) opening on a long side to turn and stuff.

3. Clip the inside corners within ⅛" (3mm) or less of the corner, so the seam allowances won't pull when turned. Notch the curves so the fabric won't bunch

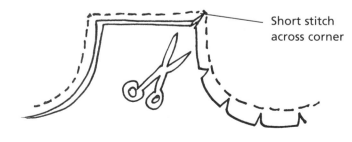

Short stitch
across corner

12-14.

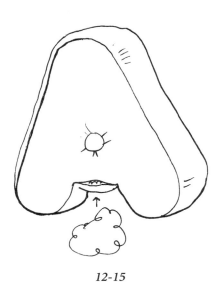

12-15

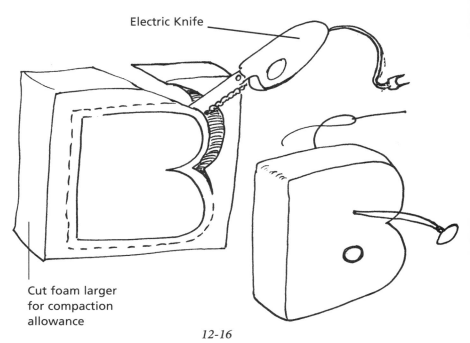

Electric Knife

Cut foam larger
for compaction
allowance

12-16

and show through the face of the letter (see Fig. 12-14).

4. Turn the letter and stuff or fill it (see Fig. 12-15). To stuff with loose filler, use a dowel stick to push soft wads into the corners and edges first. Keep adding wads and shaping the letter as you go. You must "sculpt" the stuffing carefully bit by bit so the letter will have a good shape and the surface will be smooth.

To fill your letters with foam, use a non-smearing pencil to trace the letter on the foam, adding a ¹⁄₂" (1.3cm) compacting allowance all around. Cut out the foam with an electric knife (see Fig. 12-16). (So what's a few foam bits in the turkey next Thanksgiving?) Keep the knife exactly vertical as you cut. To stuff, wad up the foam in your hand and shove it into the sewn letter. Adjust the foam and fabric to fit, smoothing the surface all over.

5. To finish the letter, hand sew the opening closed with hidden stitching.

6. Select a colorful button or make a fabric one to suit. Use a very strong thread and a long needle (a doll needle is ideal). Attach the thread to the button shank (or back). Sew through the letter, return, pull on the thread to indent the button, and secure the thread with knots behind the button (see Fig. 12-16). If this is for a young child, be sure the button is sewn on over and over so it is securely attached.

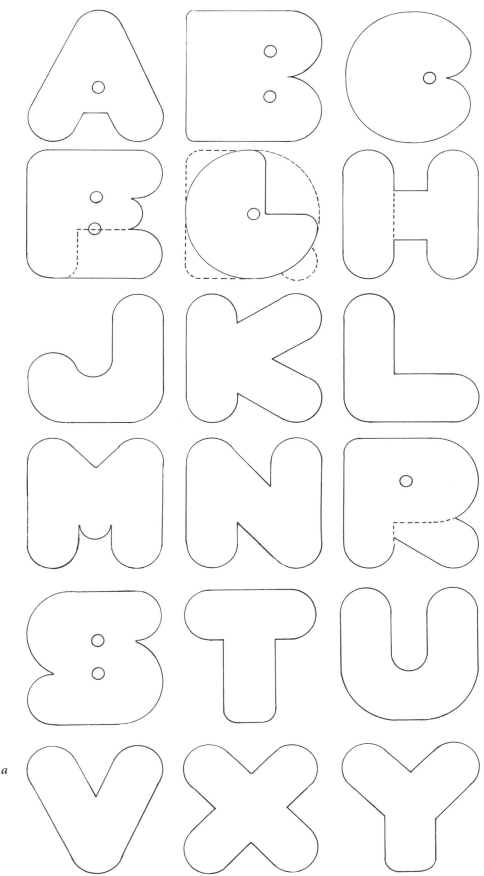

12-17. Tuba Alphabet. These fat mechanical letters were designed with a triangle and circle guide to look effective when stuffed.

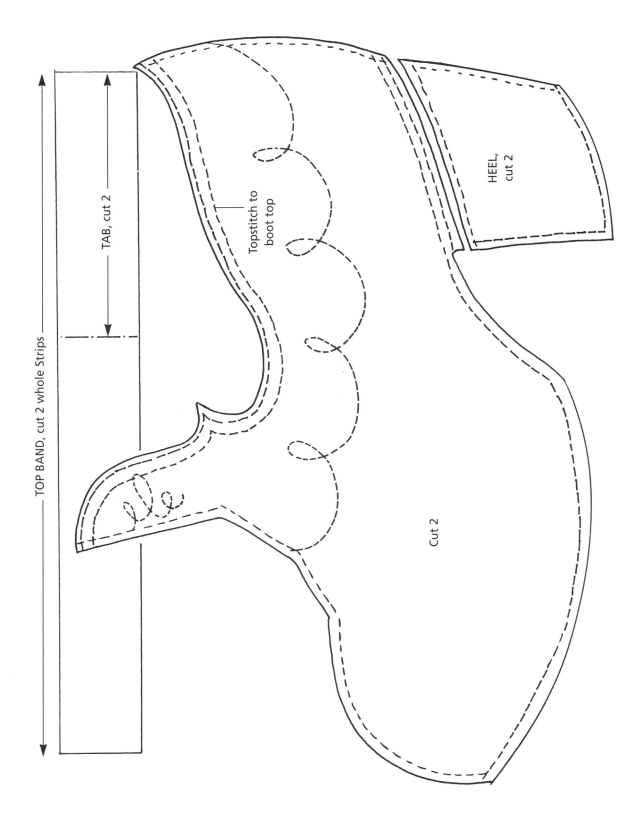

TOP BAND, cut 2 whole Strips

TAB, cut 2

Topstitch to boot top

HEEL, cut 2

Cut 2

12-18

Sew tab here

Studs

Add band across top

Cut 4

NAME

Cut Out

Cut Out

Cut Out

Cut Out

Cut Out

Cut Out

12-19

Sources
Books, Magazines, and Mail-Order Catalogs

Books on Designing

The Art of Hand Lettering, Helen Witzkow, Dover Publications

Basic Heraldry, Stephen Friar and John Ferguson, The Herbert Press (London)

Design Dialogue, Jerry Samuelson and Jack Stoops, Davis Publications

Great Type and Lettering Designs, David Brier, Northlight Books

How to Create and Use Decorative Type, Maggie Gordon & Eugenia Dodd, Northlight Books

Imagery On Fabric, Jean Ray Laury, C and T Publishing

Making It Personal, Leslie Linsley, Richard Marek Publishers

Perspective, Victor Perard, Pitman Art Books

The Art of Typography, Martin Solomon, Art Direction Books

Books by the Author— Carolyn Vosburg Hall

The A to Z Soft Toy Book, Prentice-Hall

Friendship Quilts by Hand and Machine, Chilton Book Company

The Sewing Machine Crafts Book, Van Nostrand Reinhold

Pictorial Quilts, Chilton Book Company

Soft Sculpture, Davis Publications

Stitched and Stuffed Art, Doubleday

The Teddy Bear Crafts Book, Prentice-Hall

Chilton Books on Related Crafts

The Complete Book of Machine Embroidery, Robbie Fanning

Contemporary Quilting Techniques, Pat Caims

Exploring Cross Stitch, Audrey Ormrod

Fabric Lovers Handbook, Margaret Dittman

Machine Quilting, Nancy Moore

Putting on the Gitz, Sandra Hatch and Ann Boyce

Quilt as You Go, Sandra Millet

Quilting the World Over, Willow Ann Soltow

Speed Cut Quilts, Donna Poster

Textile Arts, Multicultural Traditions, Margo Singer and Mary Spyrou

The New Knitting Stitch Library, Lesley Stanfield

Books on Quilting and Related Arts

American Patchwork and Quilting, Better Homes and Gardens

Celebrating The Stitch, Barbara Lee Smith, A Threads Book, Taunton Press

The Pleasures of Cross-stitch, Better Homes and Gardens

Knitting Dictionary, Mon Tricot

Catalogs and Sources for Supplies

Brewer Sewing Supplies Company, 2040 Janice Avenue, Melrose Park, IL 60160, (708)345-6900. Wide range of sewing supplies; catalog available.

Cloth World, Headquarters, 8500 Maryland Avenue, St. Louis, MO 63124, (314) 854-4000. Wide range of fabrics, including flag fabric, plus craft supplies. Consult your phone directory for local outlets.

Clotilde, Inc., 2 Smart Way B8031, Stevens Point, WI 54481-8031, (800) 772-2891. Threads, books, notions, sewing machine feet; catalog available.

Fairfield, P.O. Box 1 130, Danbury, CT 06813. Stuffings of many kinds; catalog available.

Hancock Fabrics, 3841 Hinkleville Road, Paducah, KY 42001, (800) 626-2723, ext 456. Gingher scissors, notions, and more.

House of Fabrics, Inc., Headquarters, 13400 Riverside Drive, Sherman Oaks, CA 91423, (216) 656-2600. Wide range of fabrics. Consult your phone directory for local outlets.

JoAnn's Fabrics, Inc., Headquarters, Fabri-Center of America, Inc., 5555 Darrow Road, Hudson, OH 44236-4011. Wide range of fabrics, including flag fabrics, as well as craft supplies. Consult your phone directory for local outlets.

Keepsake Quilting—The Quilter's Wish Book, Route 25 B, P.O. Box 1618, Center Harbor, NH 03266-1618. Quilting supplies, sewing tools, patterns, books, and much more; charming catalog available.

Nancy's Notions, Ltd.,
33 Beichl Avenue, P.O. Box 683, Beaver Dam, WI 53916-0683, (800) 833-0690. Threads, books, notions, sewing machine feet; catalog available.

Patternworks,
P.O. Box 1690, Poughkeepsie, NY 12601, (914) 642-8000. Knitting supply central for all kinds of hard-to-find knitting supplies; catalog available.

Sulky,
3113-D Broadpoint Drive, Harbor Heights, FL 33983, (800) 874-4115. Elegant decorative threads in metallic and rayon, invisible threads, machine embroidery supplies; catalog available.

Tiger Direct,
P.O. Box 569005, Miami FL 33256-9005. Computer software programs for typefaces, page layout design, graphics (quilt design); catalog available.

Sewing Machine Companies

Bernina,
3500 Thayer Court, Aurora, IL 60504, (780) 978-2500

Brother,
200 Cottontail Lane, Somerset, NJ 08875-6714, (908) 356-8880

Elna,
7642 Washington Avenue. S, Eden Paraire, MN 55344 (800) 848-ELNA

New Home,
100 Hollister Road, Teterboro, NJ 07608, (201) 440-8080

Pfaff,
610 Winters Avenue, P.O. Box 566, Paramus, NJ 07653-0566 (201) 262-0696

Singer,
P.O. Box 1909, Edison, NJ 08837, (800) 877-7762

Viking Huskvarna,
11760 Berea Road, Cleveland OH 44111, (800) 358-0001

Magazines on Sewing

The Creative Machine,
Open Chain Publishing, P.O. Box 2634-NL, Menlo Park, CA 94026. Robbie Fanning and her readers' advice on sewing machines.

Fiberarts,
50 College Street, Asheville, NC 28801-2896. Artist fiber works, exhibitions, and ads for supplies.

Sew News,
P.O. Box 1790, Peoria, IL 61656. Tailoring, fitting, and sewing techniques, and many useful ads For supplies and services.

Threads,
Taunton Press, 63 South Main Street, P.O. Box 5506, Newtown, CT 06470-5506. Articles on all fiber arts, ads for products, supplies, services, and exhibitions.

Index